3. Select books and write Extra Special.
4. Add to cart
Or go to
http://www.lulu.com/content/paperback-book/extra-special/7546365

EXTRA SPECIAL

EXTRA SPECIAL

Ivonne Montellano

Translation by Beatriz Tell

Copyright © 2010 by Ivonne Montellano

Editors: Claudia Sanchez, Romina Montellano and Bella Sanchez

Prologue's translation by Peter and Consuelo Hartman

All rights reserved. No part of this book may be reproduced, stored, or transmitted by any means—whether auditory, graphic, mechanical, or electronic—without written permission of both publisher and author, except in the case of brief excerpts used in critical articles and reviews. Unauthorized reproduction of any part of this work is illegal and is punishable by law.

Author Photographer: Mayra Pantazopoulos

ISBN: 978-0-557-30666-4

*To my wonderful family:
Alfredo, Freddy, Romina and Aida*

*Honoring the love that surrounds
our daily adventure*

Prologue

Nature distributes, in an incredible way, the attributes and human capacities to sort out the many varied forms that make people suffer, to the degree we can qualify them as, "Nature can be cruel".

People in general, are insensitive to the degree of becoming indifferent to the clear manifestation of human pain, which can make people unkind and uncaring.

Ivonne is one of those people who have spent many years of her life suffering, without complaint, living without limitations, in order to help son Freddy, who is living within a body full of deficiencies and so many limitations. She has become the most loyal interpreter of her child, who, without speech, without conscious movements, without control of his own body, has managed, with his glances, smiles, yells, cries, to live and co-exist in an active way, with his parents and sisters, in a well integrated family atmosphere.

Ivonne dialogues with her son in Spanish, English and a little French, but above all, in their reciprocal love, she can perceive his moods, his necessities, his joys and sadness in such a way as to be the interpreter between relatives and friends alike, who live close to this enchanting teenager, who is Freddy. His gestures, laughs and smiles, have won everybody's love: sisters, uncles, cousins, school friends (I know, it seems incredible but he attends school and he learns and lives with his teachers and co-students) and with people he meets in his life; in the temple or in his walks on the street and the gardens; in parties and even when he plays soccer.

Ivonne's accomplishment and purpose, was to compile and write her experiences as a mother, who shares it in an understandable and pleasant manner, and it gives us an opportunity to understand Freddy's sufferings. For his life and his happiness, for his joie de vivre to be felt, and loved by everyone; this has allowed us to learn, that despite all the great limitations and sufferings, we can always find a way to make them bearable.

This book, so full of love and compassion, is well worth reading!

Each page convinces us to reflect upon those of us who are healthy and strong, and show us that we must endeavor to help those of us who are not, to give them, and fill them, with the happiness and joy of our lives, and at the same time to learn to endure life's maladies, to overcome them and be happy.

PEDRO E. MONTELLANO CABALLERO

Acknowledgments

When one has lived so many anecdotes, it's easy to leave out a name. I wish to thank every single person who has accompanied us in this difficult but at the same time wonderful path. To all the friends and family who have a very special place in our hearts. Thanks for all the help, thanks for the time, thanks for the love…

To my parents for their unconditional support, for teaching me that love is the pillar of life.

To God, for holding our hands along the way.

Contents

Prologue vii
Acknowledgments ix
Contents... xi
Introduction... xiii
1. About pain and good fortune 1
2. A path of thorns with no roses......................... 15
3. Itinerary of exorcists, healers
   and other disappointments 45
4. My lot and challenges..................................... 63
5. More sorrows but also more miracles 87
6. About love and compassion 111
7. In painful transit towards God........................ 119

Introduction

I can almost remember the moment I made my decision. I was sure I wanted to take that step. Not everyone wanted to take on that special task, but I did, I wanted to help.

The decision was ours. People believe it is God's will that makes us come into the world like this, but it's not like that. We could choose whether we wanted to do it or not.

He never forced us to inhabit an imperfect body.

Just like me, my parents and my sisters accepted to participate. Our choices happened before we were born, back in eternity…

My life has been very different from others, as it is a passive life and my body cannot function like that of most people. My survival depends entirely on others.

Although I have no physical control over my body, my life and that of those close to me, is full of feelings and emotions.

It may seem boring and senseless to have a life you have no control over, but it has actually been very intense and somewhat amusing.

Communication is one of the essential qualities of human beings, it is vital and necessary. However, I cannot communicate through spoken words. The only way I can communicate my likes or dislikes is through my smile, a few sounds and crying. This doesn't mean that I don't have a lot of things to share. With the help of lending hands, I will make this miracle possible, to release all that is locked up in my brain.

To begin with, I will tell how my arrival was announced in a strange way. First was my mom's premonition of what was to come. I think that her memory of eternity was not thoroughly erased, maybe so she could more easily accept me and my sickness. She knew since her childhood and teenage years that she would have a child that was "different". She has always had a passion for genetics and she thought she might have a child with Down's syndrome. When she married, Mom talked about her feelings with my grandmother who advised her not to have children, "just in case"; but the decision had already been made.

My parents, who were born in Mexico, were living in Spain and had been married for almost two years. Dad had a scholarship to work for a Spanish company for six months. They had rented a small apartment in Madrid, a block from my dad's office. On weekends they walked throughout the city. On a very special Sunday they were strolling through a park (Parque Del Retiro), and I decided to take advantage of this occasion to announce my arrival in a very original way.

At the park, there were many gypsies who made a living by reading the future of the tourists. It was an amusing way of spending the time. My parents, who had never believed in these kinds of things, were approached by a friendly and well-dressed gentleman who convinced them to have their future read. Since they had nothing better to do, they agreed.

My dad was the one who got his Tarot cards read. He shuffled the cards according to the gentleman's instructions and gave them back. The gentleman placed them on a small table and intently interpreted the cards. He told my dad he could see a boy in his future and said he could see a very strong link between us. He picked up the cards and placed them once again on the table. He smiled and said, "There is that boy again, he is your child and I can see that you are united by a very strong love". The gentleman gathered the cards again and placed them on the table for the third time. He wanted to tell my father about other things in his future, but I would constantly reappear. He smiled and asked my mother whether she was pregnant. My mom said no, which seemed to surprise him because all three times he had seen me at the very beginning of the "reading". He then told my dad that this child would need a lot of his help then hardly mentioned anything else. My parents were very amused and thought it was a coincidence that they had been thinking of starting a family as soon as the scholarship in Spain ended. I was born a year later.

Back in Mexico Mom and Dad went to a doctor for a check-up. They took vitamins and followed all the doctor's instructions. They were fit, healthy and ready to start a family.

My mom, who knows her body quite well, knew the exact day to conceive, and on June 18th 1993, after a romantic dinner, my life on earth officially began.

I must've been so excited to come to this world that I entered her body so fast that she felt it. She had been sound asleep and suddenly woke up, startled. She sensed that something had happened at that instant and she told my dad, who that very same night also knew that I would arrive. He had had a dream where he was carrying a nude baby across a turbulent river.

Everything during my mom's pregnancy was wonderful. She did not have any morning sickness, nauseas, dizziness or complications. Only one time had she thrown up and that actually made her happy because she had had at last, one small symptom of pregnancy.

Four months before I was born, on my dad's birthday, my mom organized a dinner party with my grandparents and uncles. She went to the bakery to buy some bread and on her way she came across a young man who brought back old feelings.

This young man was a student at a special education school near our house. He had cerebral palsy and was walking with strenuous effort, his arms were across his chest and his fingers were twisting as he walked. After this young man stared at my mom's stomach, their eyes met, they smiled and with this they told each other more than a thousand words could say. I believe Mom knew exactly what this meant.

ONE

About pain and good fortune

The fact that I was born on March 17th is no coincidence as St. Patrick and his clovers have filled my life with good luck. My luck started the very same day I was born. Although my parents waited for sixteen hours after the contractions began to get to the doctor, and despite the fact that my umbilical cord was wrapped around my neck twice, I was graded with a nearly perfect score of an 8-9 on my new born tests.

My sickness was not due to a lack of oxygen to my brain during the many hours of labor, although it did end with an emergency C-section. I was already sick in my mom's tummy.

I chose the perfect family! My parents loved me from the beginning even though I was a very strange baby. My skin was gray, my eyes were very swollen and I couldn't close my mouth. Mom says that I looked more like a little monkey than a baby, now she tells me I am the most handsome boy in the world.

From the day I was born I choked a lot. Everybody thought I was just a fast eater, but the truth is that I had lots of problems trying to swallow my milk.

Months went by and I didn't do all the things normal babies do. At three months I couldn't hold my head up nor grab the toys that people showed me. Even though I was trying hard, my hands wouldn't obey. When my pediatrician became aware of this they started doing tests on me but all of them turned out fine. Although all tests were normal, you could immediately see that I was sick. After many consultations and much research, everybody was convinced that I had a brain injury. Even though the MRI showed that my brain looked perfect, it was obvious that it was not functioning properly.

My first formal therapy started when I was nine months old. It was a program that my parents followed from a book called "What to do for your brain injured child" by Glenn Doman. They would make me do a lot of exercises throughout the day. After months of working with me, my parents finally succeeded in getting me admitted to this program in Philadelphia. I was one of the six lucky kids accepted from a group of forty applicants. All children were checked and diagnosed, then; all parents were trained to give us a rehabilitation program that had to be carried out for six months. We went back to Philadelphia three more times before my diagnosis changed.

I remember the second time we went; it was winter time and terribly cold. When we arrived at the airport, we picked up our suitcases and looked for a cab to take us to the house where we were going to stay. It was a Saturday. On our way to the house it started to snow and the taxi driver asked my dad if he wanted to stop at a small market to buy some food because they were expecting a bad storm. It was very lucky that my dad agreed and bought some food and milk. The moment Dad got back to the taxi cab the storm became very heavy. The taxi driver couldn't drive fast; the car skidded everywhere and was unable to stop when breaking. It took us very long to reach our destination but fortunately we arrived in one piece.

It seems our plane was the last one to land because they closed the airport in Philadelphia, along with some other airports in the United States. How lucky for us!

When we got to our destination a very nice and friendly lady welcomed us; she and her husband rented a small house next to theirs to families of children who attended the Institutes for the Achievement of Human Potential, the place where they taught us the rehabilitation program.

As we got out of the taxicab, the storm picked up and we could hardly see due to the strong wind blowing all over. It was extremely cold. We obviously arrived "just in time" and couldn't leave the house for the whole weekend. It was the coldest winter recorded in the last forty years. We had something to eat because Dad had bought a few things at the store and because the last tenants had left a container with chili in the freezer. The snow had covered and blocked our door completely and they had to shovel it so we could leave the house for my appointment Monday morning.

When we went back to Mexico, we had to follow the therapy we were taught in Philadelphia. We worked everyday, all day, non-stop. We hardly left the house.

Mom's parents, Bere and Arturo, lived three hours away from Celaya, my home town; we seldom visited them. They came to see us quite often and they worked along with my parents helping me with my therapy.

My Dad's parents, Coco and Pedro lived in Celaya and we saw them each and every weekend.

I remember one day, we went to visit my grandparents in Mexico City. My dad had just bought me a new stroller. All my strollers had been adapted by him. It occurred to him that he could place a car seat on top of a stroller's frame and it was a great idea since I move very jerkily and cannot be seated on a normal chair. With this car seat where I was very well restraint, they were able to move me in and out of the car. That day, Dad had put the stroller's frame and tied it on top of our car and we drove towards my grandparents' house. All of a sudden there was a terrible noise and the stroller went flying and landed on the road. We were very lucky that there was nobody behind us and that the stroller didn't hit a car, otherwise it could have caused a horrible accident. My dad, who is very clever, parked on the shoulder and ran to retrieve it. A couple of gentlemen had already stopped and had put the stroller in their car. Dad asked them to please give it back to him. All of this happened very quickly. It was fortunate that no accident happened and that the special stroller was returned with no dents or damage in spite of the speed at which we were moving. My stroller is extremely important in my life because I cannot be moved without it.

When we arrived at my grandparents', we told them what had happened, they were very surprised. Mom had been very tense all day and thought it a good idea to soak in the tub with my sister and me to relax a little bit. Grandma Bere was holding me seating on the couch when my mom came to the living room to tell us that the bath was ready. Mom was barefoot and without paying attention to where she stepped, she hit her toe against a table. We heard a "crack" and she started to shout and jump which I found very funny because I thought she was playing. Mom started to cry and asked me not to laugh, she was truly in pain. She bathed my sister and me and put us to bed. At that time I didn't know how much pain she was in but the next morning I heard her say that they were going for X-rays and then to see a bone specialist. When my mom came back from her appointment, she asked me to pray for her because she was going to undergo surgery the following morning. It just happened that the injured toe had a tumor and no bone, the tumor had exploded and they had to rebuild the toe. The doctor didn't know if the tumor was cancerous and he told Mom he may have to amputate.

That day and night I prayed for my mom to be fine. We all were very worried thinking that she might have other tumors because it was too much of a "coincidence" that she had injured the precise toe that had a tumor.

Next day Mom went through surgery, the tumor was not cancerous and the doctor told her how fortunate she had been breaking her toe because they would not have known about the tumor and with time, it could have become malignant.

The day my mom broke her toe she had a phone call from a friend letting her know that a friend of mine with cerebral palsy had died. His name was Angel and he was six years old. My mom feels this little angel was sent out to protect her. That was a very lucky day, Mom had no more tumors and God saved her life. I am very grateful for all that happened because nobody can take care of me like she does.

All my life, I have had serious health problems but I have always come back amazingly. My body and my wounds heal very fast and I respond immediately to all prescribed medications. I also have a high threshold for pain and this by itself is a blessing because otherwise I would not have been able to cope with so many health issues and so much suffering.

Pain is very difficult for me to convey because I cannot talk and my parents sometimes don't know exactly what's bothering me. When something is hurting me I tend to move more than usual, this is the way my body reacts to pain and the only way I have to show them that something is wrong with me. They always seem to know what is bothering me, though sometimes it takes them a while to be able to understand exactly what it is. Usually, however, they don't take very long to get it. We have our special way to communicate, they name each part of my body asking if it hurts and when they reach the exact spot, I usually smile. The problem arises when it hurts very badly and it is difficult for me to smile. Sometimes we have to start the same procedure again until I can concentrate enough to smile at the right spot.

Mom and Dad always know how to solve my problems, sometimes it's really hard but we always find the right place and the right person we need. Everything seems to fall into place so that I can keep on enjoying life.

They have dedicated their lives to help me. It has been an arduous road with doctors and therapies. From the moment they knew I was sick they have done all that is possible to give me the best care they can. My sickness has been more complicated than they could have possibly imagined, but they have never given up hope and that makes me keep on fighting.

At the beginning, everybody thought that I was another kid with cerebral palsy. As time passed and I had new symptoms such as involuntary movements, everything seemed to get worse. The hardest part was that all the tests and studies they took turned out fine and the doctors couldn't give a name to my illness.

Trying to find a diagnosis for my disorder, my parents got an appointment at the Children's Hospital in Milwaukee through Terry, my Dad's "foster father" when he was a young exchange student.

The first doctor to see me was a geneticist who was quite surprised of all the things we had been through without a result. He made appointments for me to meet with a neurologist and a communications specialist the following day. This was rare because we all know how hard it is to get an appointment with doctors' busy schedules, but knowing how lucky I have been, it didn't surprise us at all.

From the hospital in Milwaukee we had to drive back three hours to Beloit where my Dad's foster parents lived and wake up early the next morning to be on time for the appointments. We were lucky to get a room at Ronald McDonald's House so we didn't have to make that long trip again.

We hadn't heard of the wonderful work that McDonald's carries out to help sick children and we thought it was really cool. Mc Donald's has houses all over the U.S. near Children's Hospitals, they help parents who are unable to pay for a hotel, providing them with a place to stay and food while the kids stay at the hospital for treatment.

The neurologist in Wisconsin ordered some tests, when he studied the results he was unable to explain the cause of my disorder. The communication experts showed my parents different devices and equipment to help us communicate, but all of it required to press a button, move your eyes in one direction or another and even to blink once or twice to indicate yes or no. To do any of the above, you have to control your muscles and I can't do it.

Mom and Dad were getting used to hearing the same answer from every doctor they consulted: they didn't have a clue on what the problem in my body was. My parents were always hopeful that eventually someone would find out.

We stayed a few more days in Wisconsin where I spent my eighth birthday. I remember we went to church early that morning and when we came out of mass it was beginning to snow. It was a wonderful present just to feel the snow on my face and then go to the Saint Patrick's Parade where I got many clover stickers to decorate my stroller.

Upon our return to Mexico, I had to go through two hip operations, and had an incredible amount of complications. Mom and Dad consulted many doctors desperately looking for help. At a hospital in Mexico City, Dr. Zenteno, a neurologist, thought I had a disorder called Hallervorden-Spatz. This disease is characterized by jerky movements, similar to mine and is caused by an accumulation of iron in a certain part of the brain. My parents had already heard about this disease and knew that my brain didn't have any iron. My dad, surfing the internet trying to get more information, found a very interesting site, The National Organization for Rare Disorders (NORD); here he found another related disease he had never heard about before. This new disorder was called Seitelberger Syndrome or Infantile Neuroaxonal Distrophy. When reading the description of this illness, he thought many of the symptoms were very similar to mine, while there were few that didn't match. Most of them described my case perfectly. This disease was characterized by damage found in all the nerves of the body. It is like having a short circuit that prevents the nerves from transmitting the correct messages from the brain. This could explain many things since doctors had never studied my peripheral nervous system and it is such a "rare" disease that even very learned neurologists have little or no knowledge of it whatsoever.

This was the way Dad discovered my closest diagnosis. He talked to doctor Zenteno about this, who immediately agreed with him. The next step to see if my nerves were "damaged" was to take a biopsy for a diagnostic examination. My parents wanted to make sure that the sample was removed properly because in the past, they had had a bad experience at a government hospital when they removed nervous tissue from my leg and when taking the sample to the laboratory it had been insufficient for the analysis.

That weekend Mom and Dad had a dinner party, for some reason they were late and there was no room at the tables where their friends were sitting. I believe St. Patrick stepped in and helped by sitting them at the ideal table, next to a doctor with whom they started to chat. He started the conversation by telling my parents that he was getting his Master's Degree at the Neurobiology Institute in Queretaro, a town that is only half an hour away from Celaya. They could hardly believe what they were hearing. They had never heard about this Institute before but they immediately told the doctor about the needed biopsy and he offered to help them.

The biopsy was taken and at the Institute, Dr. Carabez took lots of pictures with light and electron microscopes. I am sure it is very hard to find such expensive and wonderful instruments, but not so for me; they were just "around the corner".

My parents were very grateful because the study was done at no cost. They had already spent on me the equivalent of putting two children through college.

When Dad found out my possible disease, he contacted the only lab in the world that was doing the research to find out its genetic causes. He sent all the information he had gathered and the team of researchers thought I had many of the symptoms of this syndrome. They suggested that in addition to the biopsy they should have a sample of my DNA to include me in their study. It was up to my parents to find a way to send some blood to the University in Oregon (OHSU).

A week after receiving the letter from the University accepting my case for their research and asking for a blood sample to begin the studies, something happened to help Mom and Dad send the blood, as requested.

My dad's cousin, Edgar, who happened to live in Portland, the home of Oregon University, just by "chance" phoned his family to tell them he was going to Celaya for a visit. My parents asked him if he was willing to deliver my blood sample to the University and he agreed.

On the day he was flying back, everything was perfectly coordinated to have my blood sample ready. In order to preserve the blood it had to be delivered at the University within the next 24 hours.

It was a Sunday and Mom asked her friend who owned a laboratory to come and take the sample at my house. Oregon University had given specific instructions on how to prepare and collect the blood. Mom made a little cardboard box, about the size of a cigarette pack, where she placed the test tubes. Dad took the box to my uncle who was waiting for him in the outskirts of Celaya to drive to Mexico City. My dad didn't even have to instruct my uncle on how to get to the University because that's where he had been taking his daughter for medical treatment.

Early next morning we received a phone call from my uncle letting us know that the sample had been successfully delivered. A few hours later the researchers at the University phoned to inform that the blood sample had arrived in perfect conditions.

This is the way my DNA is part of the research of Infantile Neuroaxonal Distrophy. What a coincidence!

And we have more…
Good luck is with me on a daily basis.

I was almost ten years old and Mom still had to carry me and my chair to move me in and out of the car and her back started to hurt very much. We had to find another way to move me. Dad saw an ideal station wagon to put my wheel chair in, it was really big. He had to find some financing to be able to buy it; but so he did, and now we own it. Dad conceived a plan to place my stroller inside. The station wagon had two rows of seats and one row was removed to put me inside through the side door and tie me with the strapping people use for loads on trucks.

Now the problem was how to put my stroller inside. Two people were needed to carry it; one inside, pulling, and the other one outside, pushing and lifting. Dad built a ramp so Mom could do it by herself whenever he was not at home but it was not easy because the slope was very steep and she was not strong enough. She preferred to ask somebody to help her. She asked for help for two years but her back still hurt and Dad developed an umbilical hernia. They thought it would be a nice idea to install a lift in the Freddy-mobile (name given to the station wagon by grandmother Coco) but they could hardly afford to buy one with all the money they owed.

My mom went surfing the internet to find a lift for sale and one day she found one; it was a lift that was sold at auction. The initial price was 200 dollars but Dad told her not to build up expectations because he thought the price would be about 5000 dollars and that people would start bidding little by little until it reached the right price. The time to end the bidding was close and there were no bids for the lift, so Dad, with two minutes to spare, bid the initial 200 dollars and got it! When it was being installed, it happened to be exactly the type of lift that could fit in our Freddy-mobile. I can hardly believe the odds of finding the perfect lift with such a vast variety out there!

It has been a great help to all the family. I am now fourteen years old and with all the effort required to move me, had it not been for the lift I would not be able to go anywhere. It was out of mere luck that we got it for such a cheap price.

They were able to send it easily because now we were living in the States

We have found many wonderful things for me in the United States. Although I am not a resident and due to the fact that I am disabled, I was given a State insurance because there is no other insurance company willing to cover my benefits, for obvious reasons. This has been a huge blessing for all of us. Besides, I am now enjoying all the comforts that a first world country offers to people like me.

Dad brought us here because of his work. He works for my grandfather who owns a steel construction company in Mexico. To expand, Dad started to develop new products and won a scholarship to be able to market them here. The plan was not very successful but since he had already registered his company here, he thought we could stay here, being my wellbeing his priority.

Dad is a very intelligent man. He wanted to find a way to keep his company going; but it was not easy. Nobody wanted to open doors for him. He sent many letters looking for work, but months went by and nobody answered. One day he had a call from the gentleman to whom he had sent the first letter. This man was in the construction business. They had an interview, exchanged ideas and all of a sudden they realized their businesses perfectly complemented each other. This constructor had great contacts and Dad was able to offer him the structures built by my grandfather's company at a very good price.

At first this man wanted to visit my grandfather's steel shop to see if they were capable of complying with all the needed requirements and specifications, but it turned out that he didn't have to.

Six years ago my dad was the chairman of a Metal-mechanic Council in Celaya and one day he was visited by students from different universities in the United States. He gave them a tour around the shop, showed them their work and explained all sorts of technical data.

One afternoon, when my dad had an appointment with the constructor to talk about business something incredible happened. The contractor was with a good friend when the time to meet my dad arrived, he said he had to leave to be on time for his meeting with Alfredo. His friend asked him "Who is this Alfredo?" He replied it was an engineer from Mexico who he was contemplating doing business with. His friend told him he had met an Alfredo once in Mexico. They soon realized they were talking about the same person! The friend gave the constructor all sorts of good references. He was one of the students my dad had in Mexico years before. Thus, this guy felt more confident and started doing business with my dad.

This was the reason we were able to stay here and my dad's business improved for a while.

Unfortunately for him, the constructor was not a good person and he took advantage of my dad stealing the steel from the job site.

I pray for Dad and I trust that God will help him solve his problems to be able to sustain our family.

God has been present in my life through all this "fortunate" occasions; and I am really confident that everything will turn out fine as always. It is not coincidence that everybody calls me "lucky boy".

TWO

A path of thorns with no roses

When I was born, even if not beautiful, I looked like a normal baby. My reflexes were excellent. I cried the moment my mouth was out and that's the reason the doctor gave me a good grade. As the months went by, I didn't develop well, I couldn't even hold my head up. Carlos Montoya was my pediatrician, he prescribed some vitamins for my nervous system; as I was very irritable all day, my hands were very sweaty and my eyes were goggled he also gave me some medication for the thyroid gland cause all these seemed to be symptoms of hyperthyroidism but it didn't turn out to be so. When I was five months old he ordered an EEG but the results were normal. Carlos is a very ethical doctor, and when I was six months old, told my parents he had no idea of what my disease was. He suggested them to take me to Mexico City to see a specialist. He was actually very intelligent because to this day I am still a mystery.

At seven months, my mom took me to a psychologist for early stimulation classes. She had a group of children with psychomotor retardation. All the moms would stay for the class and the teacher would tell them the exercises we needed to do. When we were singing I enjoyed every minute of it, but when we had to work, I got angry and started to cry.

One day, the psychologist gave my mom a pamphlet showing all sorts of diseases that could cause psychomotor retardation. There was one which caught my mom's attention; it was called Lesch-Nyhan Syndrome. Children with this disease tend to bite their mouths, tongue and hands. My mom thought we were very lucky that I didn't bite myself although I was constantly moving my tongue without control.

It was about this time when my mom read the book "What to do for your brain injured child". My parents were convinced I had a brain injury because of the long hours of labor and the fact that there was no monitoring.

They decided to change my early stimulation class for another therapy that lasted almost all day long. The psychologist told my mom she didn't understand why she thought I could do something else, when I cried all the time during class hours. She told her she was sure I would be sitting up by myself in a week, and tried to convince her to keep me in her class; by the way after fourteen years I still can't accomplish that skill. I believe this lady didn't want to lose customers since she only cared about the money and not us.

Mom felt morally depressed with all this, but despite all expectations, she decided to try the therapy she had chosen and read about. In the book she had read you could expect wonderful results. The first thing she did was to call for a family and close friends meeting. She told them the meeting was about some help for me. Everybody showed up!

She explained that this therapy required three people to help with what is called a "crossed pattern" and more volunteers to help me with some other exercises that had to be done during the day.

Mom ended up with a list of more than fifty volunteers who took turns to come to my house everyday. The therapy was not very long; it was based only on what my parents have read so there was some free time to do other things.

My parents followed my pediatrician's suggestion and took me to a neuro-pediatrician in Mexico City. Dr. Escanero checked me thoroughly and after long time of observation told my mom and granny that I suffered from a "very rare" disorder. He gave them a form for some required studies in order to understand what was wrong with my development. Mom left his office really angry. She said the doctor had no idea; all I had was a brain injury and was convinced that with the therapy from Philadelphia I would surely improve. She swore she would never come back to his office and then we left. I must say that years later she broke her promise when she realized how wise and right this doctor had been.

After giving it a good thought, my parents decided to take me to the National Pediatrics Institute where most of the best known doctors in Mexico have their practice. They were confident the doctors would find the damage in my brain. To their surprise, neurologists didn't find anything wrong with it; the geneticists could not find anything abnormal with my genetic soup and the metabolism analyses were perfect. Since they believed in the therapy from Philadelphia, they decided to carry on with all the exercises at home and for the time being did no more studies or tests.

I was about one year old when somebody told my parents about the therapy with dolphins. Since they were willing to try anything to help me, they took me. In Mexico City there is an aquarium, called "De Aragon" where a doctor worked with what is called "dolphin-therapy"; he had great success with autistic children and with psychomotor retardation. For the therapy kids needed to be dressed with heavy pants and a jacket and if you could afford it, you were supposed to wear thermal underwear because the water was very cold. I don't understand the reason for heavy clothing because it would get all wet anyway.

The therapy consisted of three sessions of one hour daily. The doctor would carry me in his arms and would take me swimming. He would call the dolphins to come close to my head; he said that the communication waves emitted by the dolphins stimulated the children's brain. I didn't find it a very pleasant experience. Everybody who was out of the pool wanted to get in and swim with the dolphins, but all I wanted was to get out. The water was very cold and I didn't know the doctor who approached me to such large animals. If you compare their size to mine, they were huge. Occasionally he would mount me on top of one to take me for a ride, but, I must admit, I was very much afraid.

After three days of therapy, there was no improvement. We felt we had given it a good try!

To have me admitted for this therapy the doctor in charge asked my parents for a diagnosis of my disorder. Since they didn't know, they took me to a neurosurgeon whose practice happened to be in our own home town. After rebuking my parents for not knowing my diagnosis for a whole year after by birth, he asked for a MRI and for visual and auditory evoked potentials. This was the first time I went under anesthesia, today I have forgotten the countless times I have gone under such procedure. My parents were quite nervous and were afraid something wrong could happen to me.

With the MRI you can clearly see inside the brain, pictures are taken as if you were slicing different portions of it, but the results were normal. As far as the evoked potentials, what they measure is the functioning of the brain and the way it responds to different light and sound stimuli. In this study they could see that my brain's responses were not totally normal.

When we took the tests to the doctor, he studied them for a while, in private. He convinced my parents that a small spot in the MRI was a lesion in my cerebral stem, the reason for the "wrong" responses in the potentials and the cause of my disorder. This was my first diagnosis, which by the way was wrong. He said I needed to go for rehabilitation therapy. Mom asked for how long I would need it, he immediately replied that for approximately fourteen years. I wonder how he reached such a precise figure...

My experience in the Philadelphia therapy is something that I have to tell with special details. It all started when someone introduced us to Christy. She had worked with her daughter Laura for many years, who successfully graduated at the Institutes for the Achievement of Human Potential. Laura was brain injured but when we met her she was studying in High School.

Christy told my parents the moment she saw me, she was sure I had a brain injury and started to relate to them all about the therapy; how they had to dedicate all day and all their time so I could improve. She explained to them how the therapy required 24 hours a day of work but she said it would be worth it. My parents, after reading the book and finding helpers, started to work towards my rehabilitation. I was nine months old at the time.

The first program was created by my parents using Christy's advice. Before being admitted to Philadelphia we had to work with the program for at least six months. This program was both, physical and intellectual. The intellectual program aimed to teach some reading, mathematics and general knowledge using cardboard cards which they called "bits of intelligence", all of these was to stimulate all the areas in the brain. The physical program included eighteen crossed patterns, inclined planes, visual, auditory and tactile stimulation.

The crossed pattern exercise is very important because it teaches the brain to understand inside-outside how the body should move. To do this exercise you need three people if the patient is a child and five if the patient is an adult. You place the child on a high table, face down; Mom holds the head and the other two helpers grab one leg and one arm. It has to be perfectly synchronized because they start moving the child imitating the crawling of a normal baby. When you move one hand forward, the other hand has to move back and in an inverted pattern the arms and legs move crosswise. The mom has to move the head towards the hand that is moving forward. The mom's role is very important in this therapy because she holds the head and controls the pattern indicating the rhythm of movement and she also has to catch the drools that drip from the mouth after five minutes of moving the head from one side to the other. She also has to watch the other two helpers' timing.

The visual stimulation was done by my mom. She would take me to a dark place that she had adapted in a corner of our house with a black curtain. She would light a flashlight in front of one of my eyes while she would cover the other. She would turn it on and off many times repeating "this is the light".

The auditory stimulation consisted in all kinds of sounds. All of a sudden, they would drop heavy pans into the floor and would make all kinds of loud noises to get me alert.

After six months of working with me, Mom and Dad took a course on "What to do for your brain injured child" and when they showed the staff in Philadelphia what they had been doing, I was accepted to go for my first visit.

A lot of people think that the program in Philadelphia is elitist because it is very expensive. My parents didn't have enough money to take me that first time, but one day Yola, a good friend of Mom's came with all the cash in hand to give it to her so we could attend the first appointment. For each of the following appointments my parents organized raffles and since people knew they needed the money for my case, they were always willing to help. They auctioned paintings, a camper and even a car!

The first time we went to Philadelphia I was seventeen months old.

The waiting room at the Institutes was very large, it had seats around the walls and it was all carpeted so that children could lie on the floor. When you were called in, the whole family would leave together and when the interviews were over we would all return to the waiting room again. No strollers, wheel chairs or any type of car seats were allowed inside; parents had to carry their children. I remember very well an Italian kid who was fifteen years old, Enrico, he could not walk and was 6 feet 2 inches tall; his father had to carry him over his shoulders. His head and arms would hang at the back and his long legs at the front. It is incredible what parents do for their children!

I was very young then, therefore it was not difficult to carry me. The staff at the Institutes was very kind to everybody. They would feed us healthy food and would sit the children while parents attended to lectures three days during the week. We were all checked on our first day and when it was time to leave, they would provide parents with the program for the following six months.

The first program I had to follow was called "the floor as a way of life". Basically I had to lay, face down all day. I could be lifted only to change diapers, to feed me or to carry on with some other exercises of the program. My daily program consisted in eighteen crossed patterns (five minutes each); thirty two masks, a program for manual competence, some vestibular exercises (for balance) and my intellectual program. After realizing the long hours it would take to carry out all this work, my parents figured out they would have to dedicate almost all their time to me, and decided not to have any more babies until my condition somewhat improved. This was their decision, but God had other plans, my mom was already pregnant with my sister Romina, but was not yet aware of it.

The masks were small plastic bags similar to Ziploc bags with a small straw at the end and with a rubber band to hold them onto your head. These masks were very important because they would help bring oxygen to the brain. When you repeatedly breathe inside the bag, you actually start to breathe in carbon dioxide from your exhalations. Carbon dioxide is a vasodilator which opens your arteries so that more blood flows into your head. Well, I hated the little bags and I used to cry all the time but since I had to use so many masks each day I finally got used to them. To help my manual competence, they made me grab a copper tube filled with frozen water. As a reaction to something cold, your hands tend to automatically let go, and I had to grab this tube about twenty times a day.

The exercises for balance were lots of fun. They would tie a small foam collar so I would not hurt my vertebrae and then grab my hands and legs and rock me. They would also take my hands and spin me around until my dad and helpers got dizzy, but I sure enjoyed it. They would also throw me in the air and catch me, the same way you do with small babies. This part of the therapy was great. The minute they tied the collar around my neck, I knew what was coming and was always thrilled, like a prize to be expected.

The floor exercises were something else. They would place me laying face down and feet up on a cushioned inclined plane, so that with any small movement I would start to slide down. This was unusual because this was not the typical way one would come down a slide, but this was suppose to teach my body the crawling sensation. Sometimes I would slide down very fast and other times it would take me more than fifteen minutes. I had to do this exercise twenty five times a day.

I had started to grab things with my right hand. I would have to concentrate but was able to grab a pen or a rattle. After two months back home I started to lose this skill and never recovered it again.

During this time, when I exercised so much in the inclined plane, I began to startle constantly. When I would begin to fall asleep, I would suddenly jerk like in a bad dream upon an unexpected fall. This feeling was so frequent that my mom had to hold my hand so that I would soundly fall asleep.

During therapy, when they moved me down from the inclined plane to the floor, I started to have problems with my balance. I suppose it was because my legs were used to be at a higher level than my head. When I was laying flat on my tummy, my feet tended to rise and I had a sensation of falling down. I would balance myself with my stomach touching the floor, my legs up in the air and my hands trying to find something to grab to stop the fall. This would scare me very much because I would feel dizzy.

In Philadelphia my parents learned how to make an anti-rolling device; this device was used to prevent children from turning flat on their backs and force them to stay lying face down. My mom made one for me; the vest was made out of fabric with a cross of PVC tubes attached to the back. I could seldom roll over on my back, it would just happen by accident, but the vest somewhat helped with my balance because the sensation of the tubes on my back felt as if someone was holding me.

When left laying face down I would move forward a few inches, but most of the time I would rotate on an axis, my tummy. Sometimes when I startled, I would let my head down with a sudden movement. I would hit my mouth against the floor, cut my lips and bleed. Mom and Dad were very concerned but in Philadelphia they had told them that by laying face down I would first learn to creep and later crawl.

My parents suffered when they heard me crying, but they were convinced at the Institutes that it was for my own good.

Besides all the daily exercise, I also had to sleep on the floor. Dad made me a special track where I could sleep safely, it was a long quilted board covered with vinyl. The track was very easy to clean and had borders all along its sides; there I would sleep face down with a pair of shorts, a T-shirt and my anti-rolling device.

I used to cry non-stop and all my mom wanted to do was to put on my P. J's and lay me down to sleep in my crib, however, she would bite her lip, gain inner strength and leave me until exhausted I would fall asleep.

One day when she walked into my room she couldn't find me, she looked all over the room but I wasn't there. That evening she had not put on my anti-rolling vest and I had cried myself to sleep. She was very worried by the sight of my absence but calmed herself realizing I couldn't have moved very far. She thought of looking under my play pen as a last resource, she found me there, sound asleep. As I was crying, all my movements accidentally led me to reach my play pen and somewhat I crawled under it. I felt so safe that I fell asleep and spent the rest of the night there.

My mom picked me up and felt very sorry for not coming to see me when I had cried all night. She was very sad when she realized that my face was all scratched because I had been rubbing it against the carpet. My T-shirt was messed up with blood because I had badly hurt my mouth.

On that very moment she decided the floor was not a safe place for me, she phoned the staff in Philadelphia and told them what had happened and from then on she put me to sleep on my crib.

My balance problems and the startles before going to sleep were followed by violent movements of my head, progressing to jerky movements of my whole body. Mom thought that my body had started to react to the therapy and told granny that I had at least started to move. Grandma wasn't sure of this, she thought those movements were more like seizures.

They took me to see another doctor. He gave my disease a new name: Huntington's Corea. After some tests to prove if I really had it, they turned out negative.

The second visit to Philadelphia arrived and I was very sick.

It had been one of the coldest winters in forty years as I already mentioned in chapter one; we were trapped inside the house due to bad weather. Mom was seven months pregnant. I couldn't stop moving and had started to bite my mouth without control. We didn't have much to eat, but Dad had bought some chocolate chip cookies. There was nothing to do but watch T. V. Mom realized that my diaper was dirty so she changed me on the sofa. While changing me, a tiny piece of poop fell on the seat without my mom noticing. She picked me up and took me with her to throw the diaper into the trash. When we came back, Dad was sitting comfortably on the sofa watching TV and eating his delicious cookies. He saw that he had dropped some crumbs, he picked up some and a chocolate chip and place it into his mouth, not realizing that it was the small piece of poop that he was eating! We had at least something to laugh about for a while.

On Monday, we went to the Institutes. This time they didn't make me lay down on the floor. The new program was aimed to help with my movements and to bring oxygen to my brain. They made me do a daily session of three hours of what they called a respiratory pattern. For this I had to wear yet another special vest which had a pair of sticks attached to each side. Mom and Dad would place me on a table; pull on the sticks in such a way that by compressing my thorax, it forced me to exhale. Then they would let go so I could catch my breath again. Prior to this pattern, they had measured my breath intakes per minute. With this data and a metronome (device which measures the rhythm) they showed me how to breathe properly.

There were many other activities in my therapy.

I would have to work even when I was eating. I was placed standing, inside a sort of box. My body and legs were tied with velcro straps to help me stand straight. There was no time to squander. My body has a tendency of finding a way to get hurt, and this time my back was bruised from rubbing against the wooden walls of the box. I would poop, due to the pain I experienced while placed in this device but my parents didn't know the reason until they saw my back. They covered the box with foam and the problem was solved.

My mom had a chronometer that she checked constantly. It rang every ten minutes so that she could remember to place a mask on my face. She had to coordinate herself to find a way to sort all the different parts of the program. She was absolutely stressed out and would get angry if the telephone or the door rang because it wasted the precious seconds she needed to finish the program.

Besides the feeding box they added some other programs: a new vestibular program, a medullar program, a gravity-free environment, the T.E.A.S (Transient Electronic Auditory Stimulation) and a crawling device.

The vestibular program consisted in a blanket in which my parents and volunteers rolled me and threw me in the air and back down.

The medullar program was used to improve my reflexes and consisted on a very large quilted board. They placed me on one end and suddenly lifted one side to force me roll down and stop on top of a mattress which was at the other end. This exercise was done twenty times a day, ten rolls each session. It sure was fun!

The gravity free environment was a huge device. My dad built a metal structure and placed it in our living room (our house looked more like a big gym). From the structure hung some very resistant rubber bands which had big hooks on the ends. These hooks were attached to a very tightly non-stretchy suit that I wore. The whole purpose of this device was to create an anti-gravity environment where I could move freely. It was quite a show to "dress" and "undress" me. They hung me in six different positions: on my back, face down, standing, upside down, sitting down and in a crawling position. This exercise took six hours, one hour per position.

There were some positions I enjoyed more than others. Hanging upside down was fun, but they had to clean my face constantly because I would drool quite a bit. Standing was also fun. One day my mom had the "brilliant" idea of using a front carrier (the ones used to carry babies) to hang me, instead of using the tight suit, due to the fact that I was getting very hot. I ended up getting hurt with the head rest of the carrier, peeling the back of my neck to a point that my skin was bare. She thought that my crying was a tantrum I was throwing but when she saw my neck covered with blood she felt very sorry.

Now, of course, she understands my behavior when something is bothering me and always checks me from head to toe.

One day while flying in my anti-gravity environment as Mom got near me, I jerked my head, like I usually do, and I knocked her out. It took her several minutes to recover from where she was lying. I've smacked Mom and Dad many times and I feel sad because I really don't want to hurt them. They always make jokes about these situations to make me feel better.

The T.E.A.S. was added to help me calm down; it is much used at the Institutes for autistic children. I had to listen to music, especially designed with many alternate electronic stimuli, through a pair of earphones. This had to be done three times a day ands each session.

The crawling device was a special long, very narrow board (barely wider than my shoulders), about nine feet long with borders which were like rails along the sides. On the rails a small plank was placed, so it could roll from one end to the other. I was placed there in a crawling position with my feet hanging in order to push it. I hardly used it because my sudden jerky movements provided only the means to constantly get hurt and not accomplish anything else. I remember the floor of this track was covered with a sort of shaggy carpet so the children that are able to grab could use it to move easily. Since Mom couldn't find a carpet that was shaggy enough, she asked friends and neighbors for help. She gave everybody plastic grid squares so they could bind the yarn through them. It was because of the patience and kindness of these ladies that we were able to have our special carpet.

Besides my therapy, the people at the Institutes changed my diet. No salt or sugar was added to my food and I wasn't allowed to drink cow's milk. Mom had to prepare different kinds of milk: soy, almond and pine nut. The amount of fluids I drank was controlled. I took vitamins and dietary supplements.

I also had an intellectual program: Mom would teach me five different categories of ten words, twice a day, in three different languages. She would teach me the numbers with some cards with red dots and I would learn to add, subtract, multiply and divide. She would also show me the bits of intelligence, ten sets of ten bits three times a day. It really took us ALL day and no time to do anything else.

This was very tiring for Mom and Dad. When I finally went to sleep they had to look for the material they needed for the intellectual program. They would search in magazines and books, the pictures for the "bits of intelligence" then cut and paste them on my cards. They made dozens of cards with words, sentences and even wrote small books.

Upon our third visit to Philadelphia, we were taught that even while sleeping, I still needed to do work. A ten hour respiratory pattern was added to my program. For the last six months my parents had been followed the pattern manually, but this time they bought a machine which could do the job for them while I was asleep. The machine had a vest which had a pair of bags. These bags would inflate and deflate, when they were inflated, I would exhale, and when deflated, I would inhale. The machine was connected through hoses to a compressor. At first my dad put the compressor in the bathroom, but it made such a loud noise throughout the night that he decided to make a hole in a wall of my bedroom, passed the hose through it, and left the compressor in the patio.

This pattern really helped me feel better. I felt more relaxed and it taught me how to breathe appropriately, but would not prevent me from moving or biting myself.

Since the staff in Philadelphia didn't waste one single minute, they added another program to bring oxygen to my brain. My mom would help me breath through a mask which was connected to a tank containing a mixture of oxygen and carbon dioxide. The tank was mounted on a support platform with a handle. Before using it, Mom would use the handle to shake the tank to mix the gases. This was a very heavy tank and she had to do this up to twelve times a day.

Whenever my mom's friends came to help, they sometimes brought their children. Everybody had to be alert to prevent them from getting too close to the tank while the gases were mixing because it would swing back and forth and could hurt them.

It is true we worked all day; we needed 26 hours a day to complete the programs.

It was during this third visit to Philadelphia that my parents attended a conference on "Facilitated Communication". This is used quite often for autistic children and provides great results. It is also used for brain injured children. This communication uses a card with letters of the alphabet and numbers. Children who cannot communicate verbally point at letters and form words and phrases. When the system was first used, people began to wonder whether it was the facilitator (the person who holds the child's hand) or the child himself who was writing, but today it has been absolutely proven that it is the child the one who actually writes. My parents made me different types of cards: one with letters and numbers, another one with YES and NO, and another one with simple sentences. Somewhat along the lines of: hunger, thirst, dirty diaper, sleepy...

We tried several times to use them, but I couldn't pinpoint the word I needed to express my thoughts, in spite my concentration and willingness to do so my movements wouldn't let me achieve my goal. Although we didn't succeed with this technique, we found it really interesting to realize that many children are able to communicate this way; some have managed to write poems and even books. I was very frustrated with myself, but seeing my parents so confident and optimistic, made me adopt this same attitude.

The doctor in charge of the children's general health in Philadelphia was a woman doctor who was not absolutely convinced that I had a brain injury. Despite the opinion of the rest of the staff, she told my parents to continue trying to find a diagnosis for my disorder. She thought I could have the Lesch-Nyhan Syndrome, (Mom already knew about this rare disorder from a pamphlet given to her by my psychologist when I was a very young baby) and when Mom told her she knew of this disorder, the doctor was very surprised because not even her assistant had heard of it. Doctor Wilkinson was very wise and motivated my parents to keep on trying and to never give up in finding an answer.

Back in Mexico we worked for six months, but were unable to complete the program in spite of all the time my parents dedicated to achieve it. Then, my sister Romina was born and she joined me in my rehabilitation program. To stimulate her, she was left all day on the floor while I carried on with all the other exercises.

Our fourth visit to Philadelphia came sooner than expected. We now had a very similar program to the previous one. Intensive sessions of forward and backward rolls were added which ended up in chaos, like all the other floor exercises did; but that's another story. This program consisted of five sessions in which I had to roll either forward or backwards for up to twenty times; this had to be done ten times a day. Multiplying this numbers I rolled a total of 1000 times a day! To be able to do the rolls, my parents ordered a special cushioned table covered with upholstery fabric. Two people were needed to do the exercise, one to help me turn, and the other to receive me at the other end. Then they would reverse the same procedure. Quite honestly, I enjoyed this exercise despite of the dizziness.

My parents never stopped looking for a diagnosis. Finally, in one of many tests, they were told that my peripheral nerves weren't transmitting the message from the brain appropriately. When they received the results of this test, my mom phoned the staff in Philadelphia to explain my situation. She was told they could then offer no help because they only "treated" the brain and not the nerves. Thus my therapy ended... all the time and money spent had had no purpose whatsoever. There were no apologies made, we were just informed that their therapy could not help me anymore and they never received me again. Mom was angry at first, because we were somewhat deceived but later on she thought that my disorder was so rare, that even the Institutes in Philadelphia were not at fault, it was a natural thing to assume I was just another child with brain injury.

My parents never regretted what they had done. We learned so many things about the human brain and very interesting things about its development. Besides, we had met many families with disabled children and many disabled adults striving to improve.

We had met children with many neurological problems: tumors; brain injuries due to many reasons such as the lack of oxygen when delivered, when almost drowning in a pool or due to accidents; autism, Down's syndrome and microcephaly. Some children seemed to have positive improvement, but others like me did not experience any improvement at all. Children and adults injured in an accident seemed to recover their skills faster, maybe because their brains had "already learned" the skills before the accident happened.

The same group of kids used to get together every six months in Philadelphia. Sometimes one or two would not come back either because they couldn't afford it anymore, being so fragile they had died, or their parents had just given up; this time it was me who didn't return

All those years while I worked with my therapy and the Programs, I was also being treated with homeopathy to heal my mouth, to calm me down and to mitigate my movements.

My homoeopathist was a very patient man and tried all the possible medications to help me. He was a very noble man but a bit radical. When he learned that Mom also used some other medications, he refused to treat me further.

The struggle to find a diagnosis didn't end. When I started biting, my new pediatrician, Clarita, recommended a teacher of hers at the University. This woman doctor had been the head of the neurology department at the Children's Hospital in Mexico City for thirty years. When we arrived at her office, she thought I was another child with cerebral palsy, but when she studied me closely, saw my movements and my weird appearance, she gave my parents a list of all my possible diagnosis. It was a list with at least ten disorders, all progressive and terminal.

This doctor kept me in the hospital for three days, where they studied me from head to toe.

To discard some of the disorders, they did all sort of tests.

The worst one was when they extracted some cerebrospinal fluid. They asked my parents to leave the room and I was left alone with four doctors. Someone brought a huge syringe and extracted some fluid from my spinal column. Since I was moving very much, they had to hold me down because it was very important to get a true reading and not to contaminate the sample with blood. This experience was terrible, it hurt very much; when my parents were allowed back in the room, I finally relaxed.

The doctor assumed I couldn't understand what she was saying. Most people, even neurologists, think that young children, who cannot communicate, cannot understand; but that is not true. At the hospital, when I was being released, this doctor took a group of students to see me. She was explaining about all the tests they had done and all the possible disorders they had considered. She told them that my parents were aware that all the disorders were progressive and what that meant. I thought that was rather cruel, it made me very sad. Sometimes doctors tend to say things in front of their patients as if though they were not there and had no feelings.

I left the hospital. The tests' results were evaluated but the neurologist despite of all extensive experience couldn't reach any conclusion. She told my parents that she had rarely had cases she could not diagnose and mine was one of them.

My pediatrician, Clarita, was very surprised when she learned her teacher could not find a diagnosis. She had been my pediatrician since I was three, and more than once had saved my life. She is one of the very few doctors I am comfortable with and feel safe, she is beautiful, young and caring. I love her very much.

My parents were amazed by the fact that no one was able to diagnose my disease but they kept on looking.

A friend of grandma Coco gave her a book on "brain plasticity". The author Dr. Aguilar Rebolledo, was the world chair of brain plasticity and my parents took me to see him. This time I was in the hospital for a week. They did all kinds of tests including a muscle and nerve biopsies.

The muscle biopsy took months to be analyzed and the nerve sample was not enough to analyze. All that pain for nothing!

I didn't go under for the biopsies. They rolled me into another room and my mom had to wait outside. Two doctors held me down, so I couldn't move. They gave me local anesthetic in the muscle, cut a small piece and sew me up. For the nerve biopsy, they used my ankle. To be truthful, it didn't hurt very much, the anesthetic burned me a bit but I was afraid of being alone without my mom. I knew she was worrying outside just listening to my crying.

Once the tests and analyses were finished, Dr. Aguilar couldn't put a name to my disorder, but he remained as my neurologist for a long time.

He prescribed many different medications to control my movements, but not a single one worked.

He suggested some Botox injections in my legs, to relax the muscles, so I would stop moving so convulsively and to make my handling easier. My parents thought it was a good idea and I got the injections, not only in my legs but also in my arms and back. When we arrived at the doctor's office, they were already waiting for us. Dr Aguilar had another doctor helping him and they started to prepare many syringes. Mom was asked to help them by disinfecting the spots where I was to be injected and to clean the bit of blood after the shot was given. I was given about forty shots because they wanted to cover as many muscles as possible. It took about half an hour of this martyrdom. At the beginning I cried very much, but as time went by, I resigned myself. Dr Aguilar told my parents that the maximum effect of the drug was to be seen within ten days. We went again to see the doctor after those days had passed and no change was observed. He checked me and told my parents that my muscles "felt" relaxed but he admitted, after arguing with my mom, the results were not what he had expected.

Dr. Aguilar worked at the National Medical Center in Mexico City and there I had all my tests done. The pathologist at the hospital took months to give us the results. One day he made a comment regarding my biopsy to Dr. Aguilar. He told him that my muscular cells looked like those of a new-born baby. We believed we had found another clue! Having thought that the problem was in my muscles, my parents took me to see a doctor in Guadalajara. He was a specialist who had helped an acquaintance of theirs, saving him from dying of a progressive muscular disease. We were so hopeful that we took trips to Guadalajara once a week for two consecutive years. Dr. Solorzano del Rio is an eminence in his field. His treatments are based in electro-puncture, dietary supplements, special diets and other natural medication. He is famous for curing hundreds of people of some disorders sometimes diagnosed as "incurable".

Despite of the fact that we were very persevering, there was no change whatsoever.

We would drive for four hours each week on Friday afternoon and arrived to his office for the last appointment. Sometimes, when we were late, I was only able to take my electro-puncture session the following morning. My aunt and uncle who lived in Guadalajara would always open their doors for us and offer their hospitality. They always welcomed us with affection.

At Dr. Solorzano's office, he would measure my body's energy by placing a special instrument on my fingers and then a nurse would give me electric shocks on some special areas of my body. This therapy was not very painful but the shocks were not pleasant either. There were several young women at the office in charge of this machine. One of them was especially beautiful. When I was lucky enough to have my therapy with her, to make everybody aware I was happy, I stopped crying. Everybody understood and from then on, I was always assigned to her booth.

Besides electro-puncture, they performed a mineral assessment of my hair which came out with a high content of lead. Dr. Solorzano prescribed dietary supplements, special diet and anti-oxidants to balance my body. Unfortunately nothing improved.

After realizing the amount of both time and money spent, my parents decided to once again look for other options.

Upon a follow up visit with my neurologist Dr. Aguilar, my mom inquired about the results of my previously taken biopsy. The pathologist admitted he couldn't find my slides and suggested to perform another biopsy on his lab. He thought I would only need local anesthesia; however he had to put me under because I moved way too much. This time the results were provided very quickly, maybe due to the fact that we had to pay in advance to have the study done. My muscle cells were normal and they could only see some damage due to my physical condition. I had NO muscle problem; and it turns out that the "comment" which the pathologist gave Dr. Aguilar just to avoid being questioned about the results of the biopsy were not true. All lies! He never realized what my parents and I had to go through and the effort that was required to make the weekly trips to Guadalajara.

Dr. Aguilar was always willing to help me. When he had his World Congress on Brain Plasticity, he asked my parents to bring me so the best neurologists in the world could take a look at my case.

We spent almost three hours with seven of the most brilliant neurologists. Their conclusion was that we might never be able to know the cause of my disease. They told my parents to stop looking for a cause or an answer. They motivated them to use all their resources and energy to give me the highest life quality they could.

We felt happy and convinced that this was a wise advise.

By that time Romi was taking swimming lessons. Many people told my parents that water therapy might be useful for me, so I got enrolled too. These therapies were a mess, my movements were so hard to control that they had to hold me really tight and also watch my head so I wouldn't drink the water. The teacher ended up going from one side of the pool to another, just walking without being able to perform any exercise or movement for my rehabilitation. I enjoyed every minute in the pool but the teachers did not as much due to the fact that I hit them and ended up exhausted.

Always in search of new ways to help me, my parents accepted the suggestion of my aunt Marité to take me with another doctor, Dr. Ruiz Real who was treating her husband's arthritis successfully. His office was in Queretaro. Dr. Ruiz Real treated his patients with traditional Chinese medicine. When my parents explained to him about our experience with electro-puncture and he saw my violent movements, he decided to go against traditional acupuncture. He would treat me with Chinese medicines and something very interesting…with some drops made from my own urine. It didn't taste so bad and I would take it willingly, hoping for an improvement. When we nearly ran out of the drops, we would take a sample of my urine and then the doctor would process it and prepare the medicine in four days. I took the medicine for two years. Once again, there were no changes.

We tried yet another therapy which consisted of small plates made of copper and aluminum. They were placed in my wrists. In order to conduct the electricity in my body and regulate it, they had to be wet. To keep them wet, they were wrapped in a wet, soaking Kleenex and then in plastic. They were then placed and bandaged around my wrists so they would not move. This seemed to calm me at the beginning, but the effect didn't last that much.

After the treatment with the plates, we went through what is known as Vojta therapy. It achieves very good improvements when started with very small babies. We started going to Mexico City each week until we found another doctor in Queretaro. Pedro, the therapist, was an expert in Vojta and his clients had seen good results.

I was placed on the floor or on a table in different positions. My parents had to help. Dad would try to hold me in a certain position while Pedro and Mom press at established areas in my body. This stimulus expects a specific response of movement. Pedro didn't take very long to realize that my responses were not the expected ones and that the effort to keep me in a special position was getting harder every day. He told us that this therapy had only failed with two of his patients, and of course I was one of them.

We were grateful for his honesty, sincerity and professionalism and we stopped the therapy and wasted no more time. Mom had told him about a book she had on Phototherapy and on my last visit she took it to him. He was very interested and decided to attend a course with my mom in Mexico City. He was interested in his patients and my mom was interested in finding some help for me.

The inventor of this therapy was an engineer and he was teaching this course. The principle of phototherapy is based on the fact that certain type of light produces molecular changes in the cells of our body. If you carry this principle further, it is believed that diseases happen when something external alters the balance of the body changing the special position of these molecules. Isomers are alike molecules but their position in space is different. They are like the exact image in a mirror. There are only a few isomers recognized by the body. Phototherapy then arranges the molecules that had turned around, thus helping the recovery of health.

When the course was finished the engineer gave each student a lamp to use for the therapy. Pedro had his patients and Mom provided therapy for me and other people who had asked for her help. In the house that had been my great grandfather's and which happened to be around the corner from my home, my parents adapted a room with a dividing wall in the middle to have two separate chambers where they placed two beds and a tape recorder to be able to play some music. They painted the windows with black paint so that no light would filter through. For two years, twice a day and every day, Mom gave me this therapy. She would remove my T-shirt, put the lights out and place the special lamp on my chest for half an hour. We did this with our usual enthusiasm, but we saw no change in me. There were many people, who tried this therapy, but I must say there was no miraculous cure like the ones which had been brought up during the course, but we all felt certain calmness after the session. Mom charged very little for the therapy and sent most of the money to the engineer. There seemed to be nothing to help me. Mom returned the special lamps and it was by this time that we went to Wisconsin looking for a diagnosis but we came back with no answers.

Throughout my life, there have been peaceful and tranquil phases, never clearly due to a medication or a therapy in particular. My parents haven't yet found something that would provide a lasting and effective result.

We have not attempted to start on another therapy because my handling is very complicated: I live tied to my chair or my bed because if they untie me my body moves out of control which makes any exercise or therapy almost impossible. Dad thinks that if I ever controlled my movements it would still be dangerous because my body is always looking for a way to injure itself.

In Celaya, my parents found help through a doctor in the Medical Security System who helped to provide my medications because they are very expensive. Dr. Barriga is a woman doctor and she provided her aid until we went to live in Austin.

In Texas, even though I didn't have any medical insurance, my parents didn't want to miss the opportunity and took me to see a doctor in Houston. This doctor was a specialist in movement disorders and was recommended by the researchers at the University of Oregon, the ones I already mentioned.

This time we were not looking for a diagnosis, we were looking for a treatment because as I grow older, I am stronger and bigger and my movements are more violent. The doctor prescribed a medication that my parents had never used. They made them sign a series of documents since this drug is not approved by the Food and Drug Administration (FDA) and recorded a video of my movements.

I had been taking this medicine for a week when we realized it was good for nothing. My movements got worse, therefore I stopped taking it. It appeared as if this was all that this doctor had in store for me. This was to be yet another attempt to solve my problems.

During my last visit with my neurologist, she informed us that in a conversation she had with the researchers from Oregon, all the studies that had been performed with my DNA didn't match those of having the Seitelberger Syndrome.

It seems that even the diagnosis we thought had the closest similarity to my symptoms is not the right one, oh well!

Right now I am pretty stable and I enjoy this situation. I am lucky I have the help of three beautiful women: my neurologist, Dr. Richards; my gastroenterologist, Dr Behane and my pediatrician, Dr. Sperling. They are my guardian angels.

THREE

Itinerary of exorcists, healers and other disappointments

I started moving very abruptly and strangely and from that moment on, everybody: doctors, friends, my parents and even I began to wonder what was happening. My body seemed to be somebody else's. In my mind I told my body to do something, but it would do entirely something different. It was terrible! Now I have become used to that, but when this started happening I would cry all the time because I felt sad and frustrated. Despite concentrating very hard, I was unable to do what I wanted.

As time went, my body progressed to be more and more out of control. My head would always turn to the right; my legs would fold and stretch upon themselves. If I was lying in bed, this movements made my body arch like a gymnast but my support was on my head and heels. I was no longer a soft little baby and could not be left alone.

Everyday I would do this more often and stronger. I believe that all these exercises I have been doing have kept me "fit" and "trim". After all, burning so many calories has been useful!

One cold December morning my mom put some cacao butter on my lips because they were very dry and chapping probably due to the cold weather. The creamy sensation in my mouth somehow allowed my lips to slip between my teeth and my mouth started biting out of control just like the awkward movements my body was used to doing.

Despite of biting my lips, my body also seemed to enjoy pain. If I was lying close to a table or a piece of furniture my body that wasn't able to obey my orders, would bang itself repeatedly, I really tried to stop this, but couldn't. I didn't like what was happening and it hurt very much. I didn't want to bite and made efforts to stop, but when I tried hard to open my teeth, they seemed to clinch tightly on their own. All I wanted to do was lay still but that pain made my body unable to stop.

My strange behavior started to be openly noticed. Doctors suggested diagnosis that never turned out to be right; all tests and analyses were always "normal" or "negative"; friends and acquaintances suggested we should seek help from priests, healers or witch doctors.

My parents would take me moved by hope, but many times they were not well informed on the type of healing these people performed.

One day we were at a christening. A friend of my dad told him about a man who could heal diseases that medical doctors could not even diagnose. My parents in desperate need to see me get better, decided to give it a try.

The place we visited was a house like all houses, nothing strange... A very old lady opened the door and asked us in and called her husband over. He was the man with those "special" powers. He was rather old, in his late seventies, strong and tall. From the moment we came in I started to cry because I have always been afraid of the unknown because I do not feel safe.

Upon his arrival, this man stared at me insistently. Even though he was talking to my parents, he observed me all the time and this made me very nervous. My parents explained the reason they were looking for help and told him that medical doctors had not found anything wrong with my physical body, all tests were "normal". However I kept on getting worse and now I was hurting myself a lot.

After staring at me for a long time, he solemnly told my parents that my problem was not physical but spiritual. He said an evil spirit had entered my body and that was the reason I was acting (or my body) so strangely.

After these words I experienced what was to be my first exorcism.

My parents didn't know what to believe, but since they had no scientific explanation or answers, they decided to give this gentleman a chance with the hope of some improvement.

My dad was holding me while the old man did his "thing". He asked his wife to bring alcohol, water in different bottles, a sword and a Bible.

I was so scared! For the first time I learned what it was to be "possessed" and that was exactly how I felt: a body that would not obey or follow my wishes; as if somebody else was in control, not I.

As his ritual began, my eyes were covered. Suddenly, my face felt cold and wet. This man had taken a mouthful of alcohol and spit it onto my face.

I was very scared and couldn't breathe well because the alcohol had entered my nostrils. Now the old man was coming towards me with his sword in hand. I was terrified and crying, my parents were silent just watching. The old man was shouting loudly driving out the demon that had invaded my body. He was moving the sword like cutting strings around me, demanding the invisible entity leave my body in peace. Several minutes went by. He kept on moving the sword. He would pray for me and then shout out demanding my liberation. Nothing happened that resembled the movie "The Exorcist" but he told my parents that later on, maybe that night, something could happen (probably to make it sound spooky). He gave them some bottles of water for me to drink to finish the "work". He warned them that I might have a high fever and could vomit that evening; but that it would be "normal" and not to worry.

Leaving that place was the best part of the day. The moment we left the house I stopped crying. I was very tired and fell asleep. It goes without saying that there was no "green" vomit, nor fever... everything kept on being "the same". If there had been a "little demon", he did not want to leave my body.

Another friend of Dad insisted we should see a "spiritist". He would be able to tell us truthfully if there was a spirit tormenting me or not. My parents took me, to leave no stone unturned. He was about fifty years old, very smartly dressed and strongly reeking of cologne. His office was large and had pictures of saints and Jesus. There was a small altar and candles lit everywhere. It was only natural that I started to cry, my favorite sport at the time. He touched me gently and closed his eyes, and this calmed me down.

His conclusion was quite different. He said I was an illuminated being, that I was a master and that he did not see anything "dark" in me. He said I had a luminous aura and that they should not worry.

So that they wouldn't feel cheated, he asked them to try a small "exercise" for my "protection", in case somebody had put a curse on me. He asked them to light three large candles in a triangular way when they got home, to place a red ribbon around the candles and my picture in the middle. He explained that this would bring protecting spirits at night and if by chance anything was wrong, it would be corrected.

Again, I must say that nothing happened, I was still sick and nobody knew why.

My mom kept on doing my exercises every day, the ones they had taught her in Philadelphia, even while I was asleep.

Days, weeks and months went by and I did not improve. There was always a person telling my parents about a "marvelous" doctor, a "wonderful" healer...

One day, an aunt who is quite intelligent and well learned, told my mom about a man who was a "marvel" and performed miracles. Mom considered her options since she thought this aunt was intelligent. My mom soon took me to see this man, praying to God that this time there would be a change in my condition.

When we got there, I didn't like the place. I was very tense and cried as loud as I could. I wanted to force everybody to get out of the house, but to no avail. The house was filled with decorations and pictures of saints, good luck elephants, amulets, porcelain figurines and there were small altars with candles everywhere. There were many people sitting in the living room, waiting. This time the healer was a younger man but he acted as if he was a woman. My mom's sister, aunt Aida, was with us, so she witness what happened when we finally got in.

When my mom phoned to make the appointment, she was asked to bring an egg with her. The "guy-gal" took the egg and started to rub it against my body. I was feeling quite uncomfortable and angry, so I started to cry as loud as I could and to move faster and faster and kicking all around. Since people don't know this is the way I move when I get mad, they can't understand what is happening. When the man had reached my feet with the egg, I threw a great kick and sent it flying. He went pale and said: "They don't want to let us see". To this day I don't understand what he meant nor understand what happened later.

He asked a woman who was standing there to bring another egg to continue the process of rubbing it against my body, so I got sulky. When he got the egg, he started to say the Lord's Prayer in a very loud voice and continued his rubbing. I didn't like this man because I couldn't understand what he was doing. I wonder what the people waiting for their appointments thought, because of all this commotion.

When he finished his rubbing procedure, he asked for a plate which looked clean. He cracked the egg and continued his prayers while placing the plate at my feet so that "the energy would descend directly into the egg", at least that is what he said.

He kept on praying and I kept on crying and then all of a sudden the egg started to cook and bubble. It looked exactly as if frying in a pan. The longer he prayed the more the egg bubbled. Everybody looked scared and surprised. The guy-gal also looked surprised and told my mom that there was nothing more he could do for me. He suggested we should see a priest to be exorcised. He then gave mother a telephone number and a name. We left this place very much afraid, but my mom was willing to try anything to cure me.

My parents had already discarded the possibility of possession, but because of the experience with the egg and my self-destructive behavior, they reconsidered.

My mom phoned the priest. She made an appointment to meet at a church in Mexico City. It was to be a Sunday before twelve o'clock mass and there I would undergo my second exorcism; a very intense life for a four year old kid.

We were there about eleven o'clock, before anyone had arrived for mass. A while later the guy-gal arrived to introduce us to the priest. We were waiting behind the altar where priests get ready and dress for mass. Somebody went to tell the priest we had arrived but he took his time finishing breakfast. In the meantime other people came because they were going to be exorcised too. My parents had thought we were going to be the only ones present. The priest affectionately kissed the guy-gal and said hello to the rest.

All present were asked to stand and form a circle. There were about fifteen people there. My dad was holding me and Mom was standing next to us. Before the priest started to pray, he warned everybody that "strange" things might happen; that we may see lights flashing and hear loud noises and he told us that we should "let out" anything we felt, whether it was a shout, a cry, a sob, a burp or even a fart, that we should not "hold" anything in. We were all very scared, but waited. The priest put on his stole and took up a book which was not the Bible, but where all the necessary prayers were written.

He started to read in a very loud voice, demanding the evil spirit to leave us. He threw holy water all around and kept on praying. The only thing I wanted was to be liberated of my fear for all the strange things that were happening and to go home. I started crying and moving desperately. Everybody looked at me with fear in their eyes, maybe remembering the old movie. It only took a few minutes but it seemed to last forever. Nothing happened and the only noise we heard was a burp from the priest who had probably had a huge breakfast and not a demon leaving his body.

When we finished, everything looked the same, I was still sick and all present looked the same. There had been no change. I was still crying but not so loudly. After this bizarre event we stayed for mass. This was my reward for the day. The guy-gal told my parents that sometimes it is necessary to have more than one exorcism to get rid of all evil spirits.

My parents decided not to go through a similar experience again after they had been charged for this service and they could clearly see it was a sort of business between these two gentlemen; besides a strange relationship which my parents disliked.

There was yet another woman recommended to my parents. She was famous because she could "read" the aura of a person. She would draw triangles, the symbol of the Holy Trinity, and made the person whose aura she was "reading" draw triangles with the same marker she had used. Sometimes the triangles came out very feebly, others, very dark. She would provide an explanation for each color. She told my parents my aura was very beautiful and that they should not worry.

My mom discovered how you can end with different intensities of color using the same marker, just by changing the brand of paper.

By this time my parents had become quite skeptic to all these "mysteries"; realizing that people lie, trying to take advantage of those who are going through difficult times and suffering. Months went by and my condition kept deteriorating.

One day some of Dad's relatives told my mom they wanted to come and pray at our house with people who just did that. My parents thanked them for their good will and didn't realize that they would soon arrive with a group of eight people and a priest who dared tell my parents that they should get closer to God because they had been wondered away.

They really had no idea of the truth. We did not know they had come to our home for what turned out to be my third exorcism.

The priest asked my mom for a bucket filled with water to bless. I guess when he saw me he thought he might need a good bit of water for this exorcism.

I started to cry, as usual, because I was afraid and didn't understand what they were doing. They formed a circle and held hands. The priest started to pray and everybody joined him. I started to move like crazy and to sweat like a pig.

These people had never seen me before but they were convinced there was a restless spirit in me, and so they raised their voices to pray even louder. By this time, my parents knew the whole routine; surprise and shock on everybody's faces, my fear, my sobs and my kicking and moving; they also knew what these people were thinking.

After almost a half hour of prayers, they asked permission to spray the holy water all over the house. This was granted, and then everybody gathered in the living room.

A gentleman told my parents that from the moment he walked into the house, he could "feel" a very negative energy (everybody agreed); then he told my parents to get closer to God, that they must have done something "really bad" in their lives which had allowed that negative spirit to gain ground with me. He added that they should pray and repent.

I am sure my parents didn't understand, but agreed immediately so as to have them leave the house as soon as possible.

When you live in a small town where everybody is acquainted to each other, it is only natural that people share experiences and advises. In Celaya, my family knows many people who have family members with cerebral disorders and share their experience concerning doctors, therapists, medicines in order to help each other.

On one such occasion, the wife of a man who had become quadriplegic (paralysis of his arms and legs) told them she was going to take him to see some monks who could heal with natural products. She gave my parents all the information, just in case they wanted to take me there.

Mom and Dad thought they had nothing to lose; soon we arrived at the house where the monks were receiving patients, since they had come to my home town, we didn't have to travel a long distance to get to see them.

We were welcomed and taken to a living room where we waited for a few minutes. We were then taken to a room with two Tibetan monks. They had no hair and had slanted eyes. They were dressed with yellow tunics a red belt and band, and wearing sandals.

I was actually quite fed up with doctors, priests and all the people saying that they were willing to help me and never healing or curing me. With these two bald men I felt really scared because I didn't know what they were going to do with me.

When some other monks arrived and approached me, I naturally started to cry, they began to chant in a strange language, and stopped a few minutes later. They explained to my parents the cause of my disorder.

They told them my body was "paying" for all the wrongs I had done in my previous lives, when I was an evil man. It was my Karma. They believed in reincarnation and that you had to "pay" for all the wrong things you had done before. It was a sort of punishment you had to take.

My parents respect everyone's belief, but since they do not believe in reincarnation, the monk's theory did not appeal to them.

The monks gave my parents some strings of thread and told them to wear them as necklaces, since they had been blessed and would stop any "negative energy". We never used them. They also wrote in a small piece of paper the "mantras" they had to repeat like prayers to help me in this purification process. As I was told, mantras are very powerful prayers when repeated constantly; really like a chant to help bring peace to one's soul.

Once again the monks formed a circle with my parents and started the chanting of the mantras created especially for me. After this Buddhist prayer we left the room and were given some herbs to make some special teas.

This was a very different experience for all of us. We participated in another type of culture and creeds. I didn't particularly like the idea of having been an evil man in my "other lives", I do not believe in reincarnation or a punishment for all the wrongs you have committed.

I don't believe that being sick with a very rare disorder is a punishment. I am happy and I do believe we all have a mission in this life…and my mission is to be a very different boy, to suffer and to love deeply. When people see me they value more what they have and what they can do. This makes me happy.

I remember when a Dad's friend asked us to see a man with "healing powers". He had been personally healed and knew of many others close to him who had also been cured. Everybody called the healer "little brother". He was a man in his forties, and he received people in a very shabby house that was on a ranch about one hour away from Celaya.

One afternoon, Juan, my dad's friend, took us to his house. It was crowded with people waiting for their turn to be seen. There was no living room. The patients were seated on wooden benches in an unpaved patio that was covered with a tin roof to shade out the sun. There was not enough room for everybody to sit. I think there must've been about thirty people waiting.

All the people who were waiting came from different parts of Mexico and were of different social classes. There was a series of rooms surrounding the patio where his "helpers" lived. I never learned if they were his family or friends or just his assistants. They were young men and women who were kind. They prepared the medications, nursed the people and communicated "little brother's" instructions. They were extremely well organized and looked after more than a hundred people a day.

Juan had made an appointment for us. He asked "little brother" as a favor, to take us soon and not make us wait for very long. We had only to wait for half an hour in spite of all the people that had gathered there. When we walked in, my dad was carrying me. "Little brother" asked my parents many questions and he stared at me. He was quite honest. He started saying that he was going to try to help but that he was not sure he could cure me. He asked my parents to come the following day and bring a red carnation.

We came back the following day and brought the red carnation. From the place where people were waiting outside, we were taken inside to another waiting room; afterwards there was another room where "little brother" would heal you. The walls were covered with pictures of saints, virgins and crucifixes.

"Little brother" would cure in different ways. He would touch you with his hands and transmit his energy. He would use some quartz and rub them against the patient's body. He used herbs, homeopathy and would prescribe dietary supplements and vitamins. The most important thing, he said, was to change your dietary habits because toxins in food would make you sick. His recommended diet was based in fruit and vegetable juices, germinated seeds and the abstinence of meat and dairy products. This diet seemed to work for almost everybody.

"Little brother" was a very strange person; he was a medical doctor, a witch doctor, a faith healer and a spiritist. We didn't know that until we were present during his "transformation".

The day we came back with the red carnation this time we heard his helpers call him Moses. He looked different; we were asked to keep quiet so he could "concentrate". He lowered his head and closed his eyes. When he raised his face, he started to speak in an odd way and with another voice. He took the red carnation and passed it lightly against my body while praying. I was afraid and crying. The young women helpers started to call him "little brother" again and he gave them instructions in a strange language which they translated.

It seems that Moses could allow into his body the spirit of "little brother" who was the healer. People were not afraid of this, quite the contrary they had faith and were miraculously cured.

My parent's didn't know what to think. "Little brother" told them to throw the carnation in a river, to follow the diet he had written for me and gave them some water in bottles for me to drink.

We went back several times to see "little brother". My mom would prepare the fruit juices and followed his instructions to the letter. This time, we had seen people really get well. We heard testimonies of those who were cured and had been sitting there while we visited. "Little brother" was a really good man who wanted to help people. He charged very little for the consultation and medical care.

People diagnosed with diabetes, multiple sclerosis, hypertension and children with cerebral palsy would improve tremendously. A friend of my mom was cured of a cerebral tumor. This man was a true healer.

Unfortunately for me, after months of treatment, we saw no change. "Little brother" had told us from the very beginning he was not sure he could do something for me. My parents had seen a ray of hope and decided to give it their best try.

It was a strange way he cured people. I don't know whether it was a spirit that came into him to "help" or the faith people had in his methods. All I can say is that he cured many people and I can bear witness.

All scientific and supernatural efforts my parents had tried seemed to be useless. Life went on and my condition remained the same. Every so often a new doctor would see me, there would be a new therapy or medicine tried, but to no avail.

Besides my rare disorder, I have been quite healthy. I never had any respiratory complication, as most children with neurological disorders go through often enough; nevertheless I do get sick once in a while. My mom would rather not give me any antibiotics because I have been prescribed many other medications. She prefers homeopathic drugs to keep me well.

My life seemed to find some relative peace until one day I had a very sore throat. I developed a fever and my homeopathic doctor, for one reason or another, did not want to see me. A friend recommended another doctor who happened to be a nun. She gave mom her name and address so she could take me to her.

The doctor nun lived with the other sisters in a congregation established in a very large and beautiful house. She would see her patients in the afternoon. When we went to see her, we were asked to wait in the garden. There were also other people waiting there.

While we were waiting, a young priest who had recently come from a foreign country and was temporarily living with the sisters approached us to bless me. That day I felt quite ill, had fever and my throat and head were aching. All I wanted was to go home and lie in bed. When the priest came closer, since I did not know who he was, I started to cry very loudly, he was very surprised and started to ask mother all sorts of questions. She told him nobody knew why I was so sick. She explained about all the analyses and tests, how they would turn out to be "normal" and that all the doctors couldn't diagnose my disorder, nor find a cause.

I was getting very upset and nervous because I knew our turn to see the nun doctor was approaching. Besides, I really don't like to go through check-ups and I was feeling sick. While talking to my mom, the priest was intrigued, staring at me and noticing my movements, my nervous attitude, my sweat and tears.

We still had to wait for a bit longer to see the doctor, but the priest went in and asked her to see us immediately. When we walked into her office, I was sweating tremendously because I was very nervous and was running a high fever. I also sweat a lot when I cry very hard. The priest explained the nun doctor all the things my mom had told him, and they observed me while I was twisting and moving. The throat infection was checked and the doctor gave me some medicine, but it seemed to be considered unimportant.

The priest put on his stole and said he was going to pray for me. He placed his hand on my head and started to pray. All I wanted was to leave. I didn't know either one of them. The more he prayed, the louder I cried. I was so fed up! The priest asked Mom to please leave the room and wait with me for a little while because he wanted to talk to the doctor. We were asked back a few minutes later.

The priest looked worried and told Mom they believed I was possessed. He said my attitude was very strange when he prayed. He also found very suspicious the fact that medical doctors were unable to find a diagnosis. He said he was going to speak to the Bishop of Guadalajara to tell him about my case and see if there was any possibility of having an exorcism.

My mom was flabbergasted; her eyes were opened with surprise. She couldn't believe what she was hearing. The priest asked her to call him in the evening to give her an answer.

When we got home, Mom phoned my dad to tell him what had happened. He was as surprised as her and asked her to take it easy. She would phone the priest that evening. The medicine began to work on my fever and I felt much better, so Mom put me to bed.

She phoned the priest to hear what he had to say. She was expecting an appointment for another exorcism, but thank God that didn't happen!

The Bishop had reprehended him for all the things he had told us. He said people should not make all sorts of assumptions, that in order to confirm that somebody is possessed and follow with an exorcism, the case had to be extensively studied and then verified and authorized by the Vatican.

The priest apologized and told my mom that my disorder must be a very rare one and that he was sorry for scaring her. Until that day, Mom didn't know that there were only a very few people in the world with the "gift" of liberation and that not everybody can do an exorcism. It was a very delicate and difficult thing to do and it required many studies to be able to verify.

My parents were almost convinced I was not such a case, but they were nevertheless surprised that so many people reached the same conclusion.

There were periods of peace and tranquility when they were truly convinced I was not possessed, but there other times, when things would go wrong and my body would find a way to hurt itself so badly, that they had to wonder.

That little seed which people had planted would occasionally want to germinate.

FOUR

My lot and challenges

Each and every day is a challenge, an unknown.

My adventure started the day I got home.

All parents have to face a new life when they get home with a baby, they have to learn how to care and look after her or him.

With me, there were always surprises and unexpected situations that had to be dealt with.

It took my parents several years to learn how to help me. Nowadays they are experts and solve all the problems as they arise.

My days as a new born baby were a nightmare for my mom. She was exhausted because I cried all day long while I was awake. The only way I would shut up was when in her arms she paced and sang to me. She tried to follow the wise advice of people who suggested she should "train" me and let me cry for hours in my bed or pen. She never did, she knew something was wrong and she always ended up carrying me.

She was so stressed out that she developed a bad rash behind her legs that would itch whenever she heard me crying.

When it was time to feed me it got quite complicated because breast feeding took about three hours and then Mom had to burp me perfectly well, otherwise everything I had eaten would be thrown up. She never stopped trying and she continued breast feeding me because she knew how important mother's milk was for babies. Finally, when I was three months old she got mastitis and had to stop because of the antibiotic she was prescribed. Honestly this was a relief because meal time became a bit shorter, like two hours.

When I was two weeks old I started to choke because the milk would come out of my nose. The first time it happened I was lying down and my grandma Bere was babysitting. All of a sudden I turned purple and Mom asked her what she had done to me. Poor Abi, she had to deal with a hysterical, untrained, young mother and a good shock!

At the doctor's office, after a check up, I was diagnosed with reflux. I still am on the same medication after fourteen years because my esophagus muscles are damaged and don't work properly.

Months went by and my development was far from normal. Mom tried to sit me on a walker, just like her friends did with their six month old babies, but I would slide down with my soft body unable to hold even my head up.

I started therapy when I was nine months old and all sorts of weird symptom appeared

With all these different movements, it became very hard to take care of me. I could not be left alone in my bed because I tended to push with my feet moving upwards and advancing little by little.

At this time I was sleeping in my cradle after the drama we went through with my floor rehabilitation program.

I was not placed face down in bed because I would use the mattress as support to bite myself.

I would sleep all night on my back, but when I started to push with my heels I always ended up attached to the top-left corner of my bed. A good friend of my mom gave her a "sleeping belt" that was attached at my waist and with two straps to tie on my cradle bars to prevent me from moving. This belt worked for about two weeks because I then discovered a new way to remove it. Mom started to use safety pins to keep it in place but I was getting stronger and the pins would twist and open with my movements and became dangerous because they could hurt me.

A very close friend of my dad, Beto, who would visit every Saturday to work with my therapy, gave us a great idea when he told us about his kids experience with a game they played during a holiday vacation. He told Dad that his children enjoyed this game that was played at a wall covered with Velcro to which the kids would be thrown at with a special "Velcro suit". When making contact with the wall, they would remain attached.

This gave my dad an idea which he thought would give us wonderful results. He told Mom to sew some Velcro straps to a sheet and also to my one-piece pajamas in the area of the legs and butt. With this new sheet, I was then moved from my cradle to a double bed. It was great and I slept peacefully for quite a while but as I was growing older, I was getting stronger.

One day while I was perfectly attached to the bed (even though I knew quite well that I could not move, my body kept on pushing me upward with the help of my heels) I started to move upwards little by little. I didn't understand what was happening because I had felt safe for a long time lying on my special sheet. The problem was that the zipper of my pajamas had opened and with each pushing movement I was sliding out.

My parents thought I was fine because I didn't make any sound... my concentration was aimed at getting out of my pajamas.

When I managed to get out, I had reached the top of the bed and it was until then that I started to scream. Mom arrived in a second and just in time.

What she saw was an empty pajama attached to the sheet and a naked child with his head hanging caught between the mattress and the headboard of the bed. I was very happy about the great hearing sense that mothers develop to listen to their babies otherwise I could have been really hurt!

Summer arrived and it started to get hot, so Mom made me a special pajama with short sleeves and no cover on my feet, she sew the Velcro very well. She would always make sure the zipper was perfectly closed and secured whenever she put me to bed. Many days went by and nothing happened, but my body continued with its movements. One night I was alone in my bedroom and felt I was moving upwards again. This time the zipper was fine and I was still dressed. Mom never thought that a stretchy fabric could be dangerous, but my pajamas had stretched so much that I had fallen out of bed and was hanging from my waist down with my legs still on the bed. My head hit the metal frame this time and not the mattress. I had hit it so strongly that I was knocked out for a few seconds before I started crying with all my might. My parents were watching TV in the study on the top floor. I screamed so loudly that they heard me and some seconds later Dad was beside me. He was very surprised to see me hanging there and raised me immediately. I had fortunately hit the bed frame just once, but it was so hard that I had a bump the size of a peach which hurt a lot. My parents put some ice to reduce the inflammation.

A few days before this happened, Mom and Dad had left my sister and I inside the house while they went out to the yard to grab some fresh air. We usually slept throughout the night with no problem, if that would have been the night when I fell... I would have surely kept on hitting my head against the board without them hearing a sound and who knows? Maybe kill myself like that?

My Velcro sheet and pajamas were not safe anymore. Mom added some straps, three to each side of the sheet to tie my legs. They put a cushion on my waist and tied a strap all around the bed to hold me in place.

Beside the problems to sleep safe, there were also problems with my strollers that had to be modified according to the increases of my movements.

I was placed at first on a normal car seat. Later on, when my legs began to move with more strength, they had to be tied. As I jerked and turned my head with strength, Mom and Dad had to place a special pillow with a "C" shape on the back of my neck. When my arms began to move even more, they also had to tie them down, even when I was put to sleep or on my stroller.

Mom and Dad did not know at first how to restrain me. I would hurt myself with the straps so Mom "invented" special handcuffs to hold my hands. She called them handcuffs because they are similar to the ones the police use when arresting a criminal. They tie each of my hands individually and are made out of a fabric and thin foam; they are attached by a band to keep them together. They had been wonderful because I do not hurt myself and I feel safe. I have broken them many times with the strong movements of my arms, but Mom has always spares.

Each and every day my body finds a different way to move, always looking for movements that would provoke pain and I cannot stop it. The latest straps were necessary to prevent a movement of my arms that could dislocate my shoulder. My right foot has to be restrained too because its movement causes a lot of pain to my hip. My stroller has two seat belts, one to hold my hips and the other one to hold my torso. I have to wear another two straps across my shoulders so I can't move my torso forwards. On my right leg I have five straps and two on my left leg. The handcuffs around my wrists and two straps on my arms on each side are necessary. When I am put to bed I am restrained with a total of nine straps. For my legs Dad invented a support tied to the bed to keep my legs bent and apart, from this support straps are tied to hold my legs. On my chest I wear a belt and at the level of my hips they have to put a cushion to soften the strapping that goes all around the bed.

How many times does a normal person change positions in bed during the night? I suppose many, but I cannot do that. I have to sleep all night, laying on my back and tied down. I am used to sleeping like that, but I usually wake up early in the morning because I get tired of maintaining the same position for so many hours.

My movements are troublesome and tiring but on one occasion they served a good cause.

That morning my mom got up very early because she wanted to watch a TV program about phototherapy that started at 6 am; she heard me and prepared my milk. She carried me up to the studio and when she lifted me up felt I was very nervous and was moving more than usual I would try to convey as much as I could to let her know what was going on.

That night, while sound asleep, I felt something falling from the ceiling and walking from my hand to my face. It was a huge cockroach. It walked on my face for a while and even tried to get into my mouth. I didn't cry out I only started to move as fast as possible because I hated the feeling of the insect on top of me. The cockroach found the worst place to hide, behind my ear and with one clever movement I crushed and killed it. It was of course good luck because I have no control on how to move! When my mom came to pick me up, the cockroach had been attached behind my ear for several hours. Mom turned the TV on and placed a small cloth on my chest to feed me. She was about to give me my first drink when she realized I had something on my head. Her expression of horror and nausea was amusing, she hates cockroaches! Since it was attached to me, she could not pick it up and throw it. She had to try to loosen it but it started to break apart little by little. First it lost its legs, then a wing, until finally between her scream and nausea she was able to get rid of it. She took me to the bathroom to clean and disinfect me with alcohol especially where it had set. She told me I had been very brave.

This is the story of my movements' evolution, their development and how my parents have solved this problem. All about me is different from other people. This makes my life somehow particular.

When I was a very young baby I was rounded and chubby because I ate well. My legs were full of rolls and my disorder was not so obvious. As years have gone by it has become more and more evident and today I am a very thin boy although I'm very well fed. I burn lots of calories with my movements but since I cannot walk, my legs' muscles are completely atrophied. My legs are practically as wide as my bone, just covered by skin. I don't look like a fourteen year old boy. In general, children with neurological problems are smaller than normal children. Maybe it is due to the fact that our body is busy in things that are more important than growth.

During my treatment in Philadelphia my diet was very restricted, but when we left their program, my parents decided it was time to enjoy life and started to feed me what any normal kid can eat. This is wonderful because food tastes better and I adore the desserts that I wasn't allowed to eat before.

My parents take very good care of me, I am always impeccable. Mom cuts my hair and clips my nails whenever I need it. I enjoy being nicely dressed. I never go out without them brushing my teeth and putting on some cologne that smells great and makes me feel refreshed. All women, even my school friends, love to smell me and they like to hug and kiss me.

All the food I eat has to be pureed because I don't have all my molars, and even if I had them, I don't know how to chew and that is the only way I can swallow food without choking. I do enjoy all the food I get.

To be able to drink, they have to provide me with a sports bottle. It is not easy; it takes a lot of practice. My mom is the best and is very fast to give me something to drink. I can also drink from the small juice boxes with a straw because you can press them and the fluid would come out without having to suction because I don't know how to do it.

I take about ten pills a day; to be able to swallow them, Mom places them way back into my mouth. I much rather have the pills than the syrups or suspensions because they make me choke a lot.

I love the water, so my bath time is something special. Every night, before being put to bed, Mom and Dad bathe me. In Mexico we had a huge shower which my parents had adapted from a large dressing room because in a normal shower I would end up hitting myself against the walls. One day I got a big sore in my head because I had hit against the soap holder. My dad would sit in a stool and hold me while Mom would rinse me with a flexible shower head and finish the bath procedure. When my dad is away, my mom only gives me a sponge bath mostly because she cannot do this by herself.

We have now a very large tub in the new house and my dad gets in with me. Mom bathes me and dries me with a huge towel. Dad and I play basketball in the tub. We attached a net on the wall and we have a round sponge to play. Dad is fun and he always tries to brighten my life. When our game is over, my mom takes me to her bed and before putting on my PJ, rubs me with lotion, adds deodorant and an astringent lotion to prevent acne. I get a full beauty treatment, and I enjoy it to the max.

Before my bath there are some other rituals that we go through. To avoid getting water inside my ears and therefore to prevent infection, Mom plugs my ears with cotton and adds gobs of Vaseline to repel wetness. Since I have no control of my sphincters, I cannot defecate like most people do. Mom has to help me. She puts on a rubber glove with Vaseline and puts a finger into my anus to take out the poop. She also has to help me urinate, because sometimes I cannot bring out all the pee to empty my bladder. To help me, they have to pressure my stomach as close as possible to where the bladder lies, so that the urine flows easily. I guess not many people are aware of the gift of being able to go potty. For me it would be a miracle to do it by myself again. When I sill had control of my sphincters, I could defecate by myself, I would get restless and my dad knew I wanted to go. With the pee, it was more difficult to warn them. As I was unable to tell them I had to wear a diaper and I still wear it today.

There is something else which is not very pleasant. When I get sick they have to suck out the mucus because I cannot let them out by myself. I can't even blow my own nose. To get rid of my buggers, they have to insert a catheter to take out the mucus so I can breathe well. When I feel the catheter in my throat I want to throw up but when Mom inserts it inside my nose... it is the pits. This is no fun at all but when it is over it feels really good to be able to breathe well. When I get a strong infection they have to do this several times a day and occasionally use the nebulizer. When I was very young I used to cry, but now I know it is good for me and I try to stay calm. It is good to have a nebulizer at home because we even use it for my sisters too when they get sick and need respiratory therapy.

One thing that I really love is music. I could not live without it. It keeps me company and I do not get bored.

When I was in therapy, they played classical music for me, but I was a bit fed up of it so then they changed it for children's music and I thought that was a better idea. Sometimes the ladies helping with the therapy would sing and it was fun. When I turned five years old, Loli and Lulu, who are very close friends of my mom, gave me a walkman so I could listen to my music wherever I went. It was the finest idea, since then I don't want to be without my music. As technology is always advancing, after the walkman I got a CD player; later a MP3 and now I own an IPOD with more than

400 songs played randomly. I used to love the children's music but today I prefer modern or romantic songs.

Mom knows I do not like to leave the house without my IPOD and she is always trying to please me. She jokingly calls me "her tyrant". The truth is I take advantage of it and actually demand it, besides there are very few things that I ask for. When a song I don't like is playing, I start shouting so she can come and change it. The same thing happens when it's not loud enough. She knows with certainty what I want. She is convinced we communicate through telepathy… and I agree.

There are some things that I really enjoy: I like to watch some movies. I have a collection of children's movies and they are entertaining. It is harder for me to focus with other type of movies and my attention seems to wander; besides I find it difficult to follow some of the plots. The movies I like are musical with lots of colors and dance.

I also enjoy going out for a ride. Mom jokes with me and tells me I must be allergic to the house because the moment we walk in I want either my music or a movie. I love to be outdoors, see people, go to parties and do uninterrupted activities.

When we go on vacation trips I love to get in the swimming pool but I can only do it when Mom and Dad both help me because it is difficult to get me in and out of the pool without any help.

On occasions my "condition" has allowed us to enjoy some privileges. At Theme Parks we don't stand in line, so we enjoy a longer day without wait. My folks call me "Boss" because the way we are treated. When I was six years old we went to New York City and there was a very long line for the elevators at the "Twin Towers" but we didn't have to stand in line and were immediately allowed in. There is great respect for disabled people. I wish it were the same all over the world!

What can I say about my family? They are so wonderful! They make my life easy and give me all their love. My Dad is my SECURITY; he supports me and solves my problems. My Mom is perfect for me; she is very orderly and keeps my schedules and my activities running to perfection. She is so endearing!

My sister Romina has been my greatest companion during my life. She respects and takes good care of me. She is like an angel to me, I loved her from the moment I first saw her. I have fulfilled myself through her. When she learned to walk and talk it was like my very own accomplishment. When I was young I felt a bit envious of her because she could do all the things I couldn't, but I love her so much that instead it fills me with pride to recognize all that she is able to do. Since very young she participated in all my treatments and her brain was very stimulated. She could understand all the information of my intelligence bits from the program in Philadelphia. When she was not yet one year old, she would distinguish more than a hundred breeds of dogs; she would point at the correct answer. She loved art and would recognize painters for their style. One day mother showed her a picture of a painting at my grandparents' and she replied immediately: "Miró", without having ever seen the painting before, she knew the artist. On another occasion, she saw a book at a bookshop, she turned to mother and told her: "Mom, look, it is Giotto"; and truly the book was about Giotto's paintings.

She could speak perfectly at eighteen months old. She had recorded in her brain all sorts of information and she could show it off. She could read at the age of four. She is a wonderful student and an amazing human being. She is sweet, tender, quiet, obedient and loving.

All the brain stimulation helped her because when she was six my parents learned that she had a type of epilepsy. She suffered what is called absence seizures which were unnoticed, due to the fact that she filled those gaps when her brain was disconnected. My parents became aware of this situation when she commented that she had always seen some sort of luminous spots as a normal situation in her vision. Her doctor was very surprised with her grades at school and all her accomplishments when he read the abnormal results in her EEG. My parents didn't strain over this problem; on the contrary, they were happy to learn that this disorder had a cure. They immediately went into action to diminish the possibility of seizures in the future, during her puberty. Romi's doctor was Dr. Escanero, the first doctor to diagnose my disorder as "rare" and the one Mom was so angry at. Mom now understood how wise he had been and trusted him with my sister's treatment. It has been an astounding success, Romi's last EEG is normal and she is starting to withdraw from her medications.

One day Romi told me that she thought, that all brothers were like me, and later on they would become normal. She realized it was not quite like that when she went to school and her friends started to ask what had gone wrong with me. She started to pay attention to the way people looked at me and affected her a bit, because she is concerned that I may feel sad. When somebody stares at me for a long time, she looks at people with daggers in her eyes. All she wants is to defend me.

Romi and I were the only ones with my parents for several years. Mom had enough to do with the two of us; but Dad wanted to have another child. He thought my disorder was impossible to repeat. Mom was not so sure she wanted another baby, but one day, in her prayers, she asked God for a sign and something unbelievable happened.

Mom used to help at the school for children with cerebral palsy with a Montessori School program called "The Good Shepherd". She was teaching a catechism class when she arrived one Monday morning to her class with "special children". The only girl who could speak in her class, called Reyna, walked through the door came to her, hit her in the chest and told her: "Buy yourself a baby". Mom was stunned, could hardly believe God could communicate so directly.

My sister Aida was born when I was almost ten, and what a joy she has been! She is a very nice, active, intelligent and loving girl. I simply adore her and she also loves me in return. She is constantly kissing me with her Angelina Jolie's little mouth. She is called Aida after my great grandmother who took care of my mom when granny Bere had to work very hard.

I am very lucky to have all my four grandparents alive. They are very endearing and always willing to help. On mi mother's side, my granny Bere is always there for us, unconditionally; she is there whenever she is needed. She is very intelligent and loving. I love her. She has suffered because of my problems, but knowing that I am happy gives her some peace of mind.

My grandfather Arturo is a marvelous man, with infinite generosity and nobility. He is always thinking about the wellbeing of my family and is deeply in love with my two sisters; he loves and respects me. At first he wasn't sure how much we could communicate but now he is absolutely sure I perceive his great love.

On my father's side, my other granny, Coco, is amusing and playful. She is very respectful of my family. When I was a baby she would hold me in her arms for endless hours so my parents could go to a movie. She has a special gift of healing that has help me many times. She knows how to heal the neuromuscular system. With her "therapies" she has eased the pain and I love her very much.

My other grandfather, Pedro, is a very stern man but very loving to me. Whenever I see him I am thrilled. He has been an exemplary father and supported us through our difficult times.

My mom's sister, Aida, is like my second mom. She is the only one who can take care of me almost as well as my parents. She lives far from us and I do not see her very often but she is always in my heart and we love each other infinitely.

All my aunts and uncles, even if I do not see the often are always loving. I have been blessed with a beautiful family.

Another part of my family was the people who helped me with my therapy and their children. Among them Loli and Lulu had been very special. Mom met them in her child birth classes when she was pregnant with me, they are like my aunts. Paula and Mari Lourdes, are their daughters, we are one month away from each other. Romina, my sister and their other children, Maria Elisa and Yago are also one month away from each other so we all are like cousins. They've been near my family in all good and bad times.

Besides the family, there have been many people who had helped and have taken care of me. They will always be in my heart. I am grateful to all of them for their support to my parents and their effort to make my life easier. Rayo, Kari and Carmelita taught Mom a lesson and showed her that there are more people who can take charge of my everyday care. Mrs.

Anna, who knows me since I was born, has taken care of me and Romi many times to allow my parents a few moments of enjoyment and time to strengthen their relationship in the middle of treatments, therapies and stress. Each one of them has given us more than their time, it is a true blessing!

My life changed drastically after the therapy in Philadelphia. Days seemed to be endless because we had nothing to do. Mom did not want to send Romi to school and she was teaching her, so with me in her arms and sitting on a comfortable seat she would teach her how to read and do math.

When she was four she went to kindergarten, she had already learned what the teacher was teaching the children in class, and more. Mom cried the first day she went to school and, to be truthful, I also missed her very much.

Mom was giving me an hour a day of phototherapy, but there were still many hours to fill.

My aunt Geor thought that I could go and learn catechism, so we went to see Telis, the lady in charge of the programs at "The Good Shepherd".

The volunteers were teaching at a large house where "normal" children would attend school. Children with some neurological disorder were taught at a different facility. For a reason I don't know, I was placed with the children at the large house and not with the ones with cerebral palsy. Romi and Mom came with me. My sister would take the class with me while Mom helped the teachers. On Tuesdays Mom would attend a class to learn how to teach the program and thus she became a volunteer for the special children.

After a year of going to "The Good Shepherd" I started to prepare for my First Communion. I enjoyed the presentations and all the material they had for the lessons. I would attend to these classes with all the other children who were having their First Communion. Telis realized that I would adapt better when I was alone and not with my mom. I think this is a normal reaction in all children. Mom never thought I could go to school because I was always crying and my care is complicated, to say the least; but Telis opened my mom's eyes. I owe her the happiest years of my life.

Hanging out with all the children was really cool. At the beginning they would look at me with curiosity but, little by little they got used to me and I got used to them. Before our First Communion we went to a retreat and everybody would help me with all the crafts. Everyone wanted to push my stroller along the aisle in church that day. I really felt loved.

It was a very hot day and all the children were wearing a white tunic but I was dressed in shorts and a white T-shirt because I was sweating a lot. My tunic was hung on my stroller only as a symbol. We were formed on line and the kid who pushed my stroller in the aisle was the tallest so we were the last ones to parade. The church was full and they were playing my favorite song: "God is here". I was at my favorite place! I saw the faces of family and friends; some of them with tears in their eyes.

I was so in peace despite of the heat and behaved well until the celebration ended. Every so often I would get nervous but my godfather, Edwin, tickled me on my palms and that soothed me. There were fifteen of us. The priest was very excited when he came to me to give me Communion. He said: ""now is the great moment". It was incredible! Faith has kept me going and knowing that Jesus was in me, near me, was a magical moment.

To this day, my parents always take me to church on Sundays. I very much enjoy being in God's house. During mass, we line up to receive Communion. This is my weekly reward, being able to talk to Jesus.

I love my parish, Saint Thomas More church here in Austin. The priests are true God's men and the community is completely dedicated to service. The people there are loving and caring to me, they make me feel welcome.

After our experience with my First Communion friends, Mom decided to follow Telis' advice and give the school a try. She didn't want a special education school because she knows I love to be with normal children, so she started to look for a place where they would integrate disabled children in their normal classes. Even though this is the law in my country, very few schools do it.

There was the principal at one of the schools who didn't want to deny my mom and recommended a teacher who had a lot of experience integrating children with disabilities.

What a blessed day it was when Mom met my teacher, Carmelita Llaca!

She had been a teacher for many years and decided to open her own school where ALL children were welcomed. I was accepted immediately under no conditions or exceptions. I was treated the same way all children are treated in school. To get started my parents had to buy all the school material that was needed. I knew I couldn't hold them with my own hands, but yet I was proud to have my own things, just like everybody else.

My first day in school was rather complicated for my mom and me. The teacher had given her permission to come and see me every hour because we all had to learn; the teachers, how to deal with me and I, had to learn to accept a very different atmosphere. Mom left me with a gap in her heart. She couldn't have imagined that one hour later a problem would arise. It was about lunch time when my mom left and then we left the classroom. The teacher, Blanca, who was also a nurse, thought it a good idea to let me lie down on a blanket to relax from my chair. When I felt unstrapped I started to get nervous and couldn't understand how Mom had forgotten to tell the teachers never to move me out of the chair. We had a real battle; the moment I felt free, I started to move as usual, but the teacher who knew nothing of my problems, couldn't hold me. Being afraid that she would be unable to hold me and therefore drop me, I began to move even more earnestly. Fortunately, Mario, Mrs. Carmelita's son, was there and both of them were finally able to restrain me. They decided to sit me back on my chair instead of on the floor, which was a very wise decision. It was difficult for them to tie and restrain me, but they did it the best they could.

Mom arrived to see me just then. When they told her about our big adventure, she realized she had to warn them about my movements. She explained to my teacher Carmelita all the details of my condition and from then on she didn't come back to see me each and every hour. She would drop me at 10 am and pick me up at 1 pm.

Patty was another teacher at that school. She learned how to give me my juice and help me if I choked. Sometimes when I turned purple she was scared, but stayed cool and she was with me until I started to breath normally.

I had my good and my bad moments during the years I spent in this school. Sometimes I missed school because I was sick or in hospital but I was always welcomed. When I got back, they were caring and treated me with so much respect. The kids in school missed me and were happy to see me back.

All the years I spent in this school taught me to be more tolerant and to learn to share. They were incredible. I had fun with my friends. When we had a break we would play soccer. I was chosen to be the goalie and I didn't care even if I was hit with the ball. At times, when I was bored in my classroom, I would shout and then Patty would come for me and take me to her classroom. Most of the times I was fine but whenever I felt nervous they would know how to care and sooth me. I enjoyed the festivals and theater. I was part of all events as well as all the other disabled children who had found a true home there.

The day I left, they gave me my diploma and a certificate for succeeding in finishing my elementary school.

When we moved to Texas, we went to see the middle school where I was going to start my 7th grade. This is equivalent to secondary school in my country. In the USA all children have the right to education, even disabled children. My new school is huge, just their administration office is as large as my whole school in Celaya. The school has a very large room especially designed for special children. There are four teachers for six students. Mrs. Aline Crompton, who is the teacher in charge, talked to my mom and told her she would take care of me. Mom was concerned because it was a big change, she had thought it was going to be like the school in Mexico, that I would stay for three hours, which is the right length of time for me and I do not need a change of diapers. Aline told my mom that school started at 8:30 am and ended at 4 pm. She was going to see about all my needs including my feeding and change of diapers. She added she had two children and that she was going to take care of me as if I was her child too. Nobody had taken my supervision without my mom being present. She had never been separated from me for that long and I saw her cry.

The first day of school arrived! A bus came to pick me up at my door with two ladies who were in charge of the children. Mrs. Dixie was the driver, and Mrs. Jackie, the monitor. Mrs. Jackie was the one to secure my chair with special straps in the bus. The bus has a lift similar to the one we have in our station wagon. All year I went to school by myself because Romi was still in elementary school.

I must admit I was nervous at first, but when I arrived, everybody was nice to me and I started to taste my new good life.

My mom came to school several times to show the teachers how to restrain me, how to feed me and how to change my diaper. I missed Mom but I was proud of having my own activities without her watching me all day long.

My teachers are great and take excellent care of us. They are patient and teach us well.

Crompton is a tall, strong lady very caring and has come to know me very well. She knows how to deal with me and is not scared when I choke. She makes me feel safe and I love her very much.

The school has been great. I take most of the lessons in a classroom and I also participate in many other activities with the rest of the kids. I enjoy my theater art and social studies classes. When I am taken to the cafeteria I can look at the girls who are very pretty. Some of the girls ignore me, but some others are endearing. Crompton prefers to feed me in the classroom, which I think is better. Romina, my sister, now comes to the same school with me and she visits and checks me. She has made friends with all my class mates. Every day

Mrs. Jackie comes with her husband Bob who is our new driver to pick us up and they deliver us back home about 5 pm.

My classmates are fun. I am the only one who cannot walk. Some of my class mates cannot talk and others utter noises only. I enjoy seeing my friends misbehave. Crompton says that I would be a very mischievous kid if I could. She is right.

My autistic friends are geniuses. They communicate through facilitated communication and they are excellent in science. Mike, a friend of mine, won a prize at the Science Fair Competition in Austin and was among the best in Texas competing with normal children.

Every Friday they take us out for a ride. This activity I enjoy very much. What I enjoy most is bowling. I never thought I could be able to play this game, but here they have these nice ramps and with them the only thing you have to do is give the ball a good hit; of course I can do that. I would like to participate in the Special Olympics some day. This event is organized every year and is really cool.

Being away from my family for so many hours, I have shared the lives of many young people and I have learned to be patient and tolerant. I am not the King here, I am just another student and I am addressed like everybody else. These two years have been excellent, but now a new change is coming.

Next year I have to change schools and get to High School. When summer is over I have to adapt to new school mates and teachers.

I understand it will be difficult at first but I have learned that there are many people who can help me. What seemed to be impossible has been accomplished and we've learned a nice lesson. I shall go to the new school and I shall adapt little by little. People would get to know me and I shall keep on being very happy.

FIVE

More sorrows but also more miracles

I had been in my cast for three months and the heat inside was unbearable. I would sweat all day even though I had no clothes on, only my diaper. The plaster weighed a ton and made me feel like I was in an oven all day long.

Grandma Bere loves astrology, and as many others, she believes that the planets have influence over our lives. I really do not doubt it, since the oceans rise and fall with different tides all because of the moon. Why should it not be true?

She had gone to see an astrologist five months before, and she was told that my mom and I had bone problems. Grandma knew about my mom's backache because she would carry my chair in and out of the car all the time. The chair added about twenty pounds to my weight, but Grandma was surprised when she heard that I also had bone problems. About a week later my parents noticed that my femur was completely dislocated.

That was the beginning of the worst time of my life.

Mom and Dad took me to see the bone specialist. No X-rays were necessary, it was quite obvious. Nevertheless, they took an X-ray to confirm. They found my hip-joint dislocated, that is to say, my bone had come out of the socket.

The doctor said he did not recommend the operation because the recovery was a long and difficult one and he knew many people who live without pain despite this condition. We left his office convinced of this. Unfortunately, what followed was not what the doctor had predicted because, due to my violent movements, the pain in my hip became unbearable! What made it worse was that the more it hurt, the more I moved. I could not stop the pain, whether I was sitting or lying down, not even in my parents' arms, it became stronger and stronger.

I remember the day we went to see another doctor, the one who performed the surgery. It was just Mom and I, and we waited for many hours for our appointment. Dr. Quintana was a young and very presentable man and since he was the son of Dad's friend, I felt nothing could go wrong. My mom gave him my X-rays and the doctor showed her some other X-rays from children who had gone through the same operation. He explained the procedure and truly gave us confidence in his abilities. Still Mom expressed concern about my problem with the involuntary movements and how pain provides stimulus for my body to keep injuring itself. He figured there would be no problem because of a soft cotton fabric which he informed was to be placed between the cast and the skin. He said, everything would turn out fine.

We were concerned with the operation and recovery period, but there was no other option but to fix my dislocated bone. On April 3rd, 2002, I entered the operating room for the procedure. It was very cold and I was absolutely terrified. I wanted my mom and dad to be with me. Although it was not my first time to be operated on or anesthetized, it was the first time for such a delicate surgery. I knew Dr Colin quite well; he had been the anesthesiologist at the time when my teeth were extracted. He was very kind, and in spite of my desperate cries, he spoke to me with a soft voice and told me what he was doing. He placed a mask with a familiar but strong odor on my face. I became dizzy and don't remember anything until I awoke.

The wait seemed like an eternity to my parents. After five hours, the doctor came out to tell them that the operation had been successful, and that I was fine. My parents greeted me and went with me to my hospital room. My mom knew, as soon as she saw me, that something was very wrong...

The pain I was feeling now was not comparable to the pain I had the weeks before the operation. This time it was unbearable. From the moment I woke up from the anesthesia, I felt the cast against my body and I started to move (this is something my body does and over which I have no control). There was indeed a sort of fine cotton inside the cast, but the fabric was so thin and my hip movements were so violent that this served no purpose. I was sure my mom knew what was happening; she knew that inside the cast I felt a pain burning like fire, and about a thousand thorns rubbing against my skin. She asked a friend to bring her some fabric to cushion the edges of the cast. The rubbing of the cast against my waist and back was hurting my skin. She did not dare put anything inside the cast because she knew I had an open wound from the surgery.

My room at the hospital was well lit and I could hear the sounds of cars driving by on the street and of the children chatting as they left school. My dad helped the nurse move me from the stretcher to my bed and adjust my IV Mom tried her best to comfort me. She would come close to me and caress me whispering: "don't worry, Mom is here". Her voice and warmth made me feel better, but I was desperate. I tried to tell her that I was in pain and I this pain was unbearable. I wanted to ask her for help, but I was unable to do it and this made me very sad. My dad would hold my hand and look at me tenderly. People came in and out of the room all the time. Friends and family came to see how I was doing, and all I wanted was for the pain to go away.

The nurse placed a gadget which looked like strips of wood covered with adhesive tape to hold my IV in place. This is normally used with children who move or toss so that they cannot hurt themselves or have the needle come out of place. Things that work for others, never work for me...

The pain was getting to be unbearable; each and every movement would rub the skin over my hip bones. This constant rubbing lifted the skin until I had nothing left but raw flesh. And still, I could not stop moving.

When Dr. Quintana came to see me, my mom was grief-stricken. She could not see how hurt I was inside, but she could see what was happening to the cast outside and imagined how this must be affecting my newly set bones. The doctor could hardly believe what he was seeing. My body strength was so great that the fresh cast which had not entirely dried was breaking in the middle. The strength of the downward movement of my legs, despite of being also in a cast, had broken the cast at my groin level. Mom had warned the doctor of this possibility when we first visited him at his office; but he did not believe I was capable of having such great strength. He did not believe my pediatrician, Clarita, either when she had called to advise him to take my movements into account before he operated on me.

Besides the pain from the trauma of my operation, and the pain of my skin rubbing against the cast, now my hand started to burn horribly. The gadget they placed for my IV had not helped and with the needle out of place, the solution was not going into my vein. By the time they noticed what had happened; my hand looked like an inflated balloon. They immediately removed the IV and the relief I felt was incredible. It didn't matter that they had to give me more and other oral medicines. I was rid of one pain and therefore willing to accept anything.

When I left the hospital, we went directly to the doctor's office where he placed a plastic bandage around my cast. The plastic was unbreakable and although light, it did add a few ounces to the cast. I now needed two people to carry me. Dad, who is an engineer, placed some aluminum bracings above and under my legs to further prevent the cast from breaking. From this moment on, my parents began what were to be the endless visits to doctors' offices and operating rooms!

I was covered with a cast, plastic bandages and aluminum strips from my waist down. I was in a strange posture; my legs were bent and separated with a stick in the middle so I could be carried. My butt and penis were uncovered so they could change my diapers and clean me. I would still sweat like as being in a sauna and this small ventilation did not help much.

When Mom saw the first X-ray she was mortified! I heard her say to my dad in tears: "What did we do? This is the beginning of the end..." Dr. Quintana had forgotten to disclose a small detail about the surgery. In order to set the bone in place, it had to be broken at first, and then once in place, joined with screws and metal plates. He had ignored my parents' information about my jerky and violent movements, the tremendous strength, and the possible consequences.

The days that followed were a nightmare, not even the morphine eased the pain. My wounds burned like an open fire. The sores on my hip were getting deeper so my parents decided to cut the cast and bandages around the hip bones to be able to reach my wounds so they could be healed. They knew my skin was really hurt but were shocked when they found out my sores were so deep that my bones could be seen. Now my parents had to spray the wounds with an anesthetic so as to wash and apply the medications, but the pain from the spray itself made me faint. An X-ray was taken to see if the plates and screws were in place, but my mom was right when she said "this is just the beginning…"

The X-ray showed the metal plates were loose. In addition, out of the two large screws used to stabilize my bone, one of them was now dangerously close to my bladder and could perforate it. I was feeling terribly sick, tired of the weight of the cast. I had been like this for fifteen days and my wounds would not heal. The daily treatments were painful. The water I drank wasn't enough because I was constantly sweating. I was not hungry, slept very little at night and would doze all day. I was becoming weaker and weaker and since I was hurting, I kept moving constantly.

I had to be taken to the hospital where my dear pediatrician, Clarita, took over my care and tried to make me stronger. I underwent another operation because the femur was fractured and the plates and screws were loose. My condition was considered "critical". I was eight years old, I had lost so much weight. I now weighed only twenty pounds! I was completely dehydrated, my blood was weak and my bone had a large break.

Clarita knows me well. The first thing she ordered was a venous-dissection. When I heard such a word I started shaking, it sounded painful. It turned out to be something not very pleasant but, it saved me from future problems. As Dr. Montoya arrived; he tied my arm tightly to the bed and asked my mom to help him. He then gave me a shot that burned a little but I soon realized it was local anesthesia since I didn't feel any of the other things he did. He cut my arm near a vein, carefully brought it out and placed a small metal stick underneath to support it so it would not get inside my arm again. He made a hole in the vein and then inserted a very thin but very long catheter. He informed my mom that inside my body, it reached up to the level of my neck. After he inserted the catheter, he carefully closed the vein and my arm. This had to be done to avoid any problems with the IV fluid and even if I moved as usual, the medication could get directly into my system.

I had to be operated on promptly, so they gave me a blood transfusion, IV fluid and medication. I was so weak that fungi had invaded my body, from my mouth to my anus. It seemed like I was never going to heal. I didn't know what to think. I trusted my pediatrician, my parents and above all I trusted God. I did not want to die. I wanted to recover soon, so I prayed for God to help me.

Clarita came the following morning with excellent news from the lab. She came in shaking a piece of paper in her hand and told my mom that a miracle had happened. The transfusion had been successful and my blood was stronger. I now could have the operation. We were happy with the good news but the thought of surgery gave us the chills. We knew it was an absolute must.

Dr. Quintana scheduled the operation for the next day, at eight o'clock in the morning. I was very nervous that afternoon. I didn't want to go through the same situation again. I felt confident though. My parents had asked the doctor to place a layer of foam between the cast and my skin, and were also allowed to be present during my surgery. The doctor had agreed to do this since he had seen how badly I was hurt.

Many people came to see me, friends and family, all carrying fruits or food because my parents never left my side. They even ate in my room. They became skinnier everyday, just like me.

Grandma Bere, was looking after my sister Romina so that my parents could stay with me. Dad didn't even go to work.

I remember that Rayo came to see me. She was the nurse my parents had hired to help Mom at home. At the beginning she did nothing because my mom wouldn't let her, since she was so used to do everything for me, she thought nobody else was capable of doing it. My mom would bathe me with a sponge, give me my medications and feed me. Rayo only watched. One day Mom had to leave the house and when she came back she realized Rayo had done everything perfectly well. That was a very good day because Mom realized she could trust somebody else with my care. From that day on, things became easier for her. I was very pleased she could finally relax a bit. Rayo became a part of our family. She is a wonderful girl and we love her. I was very happy when she dropped by at the hospital to see me.

Later on, Araceli the nurse came to check my IV The bad news for the day was that it was plugged but she was patient enough to unplug it. She was aware it was a venous-dissection and wanted to save me from a "repeat" procedure. It took her more than half an hour, but she finally did it. My mom was very grateful with her for saving me from even more pain.

Dr. Quintana is the least punctual person I've ever met. Dr Colin hates this because he is very organized. As an anesthesiologist he has a full agenda but he is always on time.

That day we were really thankful about his lack of punctuality!

I was going into the operating room at 7:30 a.m. to be prepared and ready, but Dr. Quintana didn't show up on time. Dr. Colin had been waiting patiently, but an hour later he was quite upset. When two hours had gone by, he got really angry, but was kind enough to stay because he understood my condition.

My parents and I were waiting in my room, and as time passed we were getting very nervous. All of a sudden Dr Colin came into the room and told my dad he had something important to discuss with him. When Dad came back, we couldn't believe the story he told us.

While we were waiting for Dr. Quintana in my room, a lady had arrived to the emergency room with an incredible stomach ache. Her family had brought her to the hospital after a few days of pain. She was admitted to the ER and the doctor in charge had to take her to the operating room immediately because she had peritonitis. When the doctor opened her stomach, it literally exploded! She had such a large amount of gas that it was like a bomb, ready to burst. When it exploded, all the gas, fluids, blood and all sorts of bacteria came out contaminating all the nurses' uniforms, doctors, furniture and instruments; let's just say the entire environment.

My operation was scheduled at exactly the same time this lady exploded in the operating room. Had I been there exposed to all these bacteria and microbes with my open wounds and as weak as I was, it would have infected me and could have been terrible. The contamination was so bad that it invaded three operating rooms which were next to one another.

We had to wait a full day for the room to be cleaned and sterilized. Nobody ever complained about Dr. Quintana's lack of punctuality, not even Dr. Colin.

The dreaded day had arrived! Everybody was on time. I felt terrified but more confident since my parents would be near me. Dr. Colin put the mask over my face and I don't remember anything else.

When I awoke, I was still in the operating room. I saw my parents all dressed with blue gowns and head coverings, just like the doctors. I was very dizzy and the wound from the surgery was very painful. I was covered with the plastic bandage but I had a cushion inside. My parents had cut pieces of foam so that the doctor could place them between the bandage and my cast. Later on Mom told me they had closed my sores by sewing them. I felt safer.

I heard the doctors say the surgery had gone well. The dangerous screws were removed to avoid any perforation. Also the screws and plates were removed and replaced by three huge pins holding the bones from the inside; there was no way possible that they could move out of place.

Everything seemed to have been a real success, but I continued moving even with the cast. I had the foam inside to protect me but with all the pain I couldn't stop.

To change my position, they placed me on my chair to move me from the bed. Dad had adapted it so I could sit down; it was very thoughtful of him. I was growing tired of lying down on the bed all the time.

That afternoon I looked better and felt better, so Mom went to see my sister, Romi. Dad told her he would stay with me, and not to worry. When Dad and I were alone, he carried me back to the bed. Inside the cast I started moving so violently that when he laid me down, I felt a stabbing pain inside my body, so bad I cannot describe. Dad must have seen something in my face because he panicked. The pain was so strong that I started to sweat cold and my eyes were wide open and fixed, with a blank stare. At that moment God sent an angel, Clarita, and when she saw me as pale and sweaty she knew something was wrong. She listened to my heart rate and took my pressure (I hardly had any). I was in shock. Clarita knew I had an internal hemorrhage. Dad moved me from the bed back to the seat. The nurses rushed in and out. Clarita was telling them what to do, I was given some shots and two platelet bags were placed into my IV to hold the bleeding. If Clarita had not arrived the moment she did, I would not be telling my story right now. I thank God for sending her to me.

Everything seemed to be under control; Dad phoned Mom and told her what had happened. She rushed back to the hospital. It was such a relief for me to see her.

My sister's sixth birthday was the following day. My aunt Aida and my cousin Diego had come to Celaya to see me and to wish her Happy Birthday. All Romi wanted was to come to the hospital to visit me, and when she saw me, her eyes filled with tears. I was no more than a bag of bones, very pale, with an IV and a cast. She let out a sigh and said: "Poor Freddy" with such sadness that I could feel it in my heart.

They took her out to eat to celebrate her birthday, but she could care less. She had left her heart with me, in my cold room at the hospital. She knew that having seen her had filled me up with joy.

I spent that night at the hospital. The following day I was to be released. To verify everything was in order, they took some X-rays. Dr. Quintana was very busy and he sent his assistant instead.

By this time, Mom had seen so many X-rays that she could read them and what she saw broke her heart. I heard her cry in despair, like never before. Dr. Quintana's assistant was paralyzed. She saw that the large pins that "were not to fail", had broken the thin wall of my bone, they were out of place and had split my femur in two again. The night before, when I had been in shock and Clarita saved me, was the exact moment I had fractured my femur, causing the hemorrhage and the reason for such a terrifying pain.

My mom was out of control, there was no power on earth to make her stop crying. I didn't understand what was happening and all I wanted was to go home.

Dr Quintana finally decided to show up and see for himself, what his assistant had reported on the phone. Very coldly and with an icy tone in his voice he told my parents that he would think about a way to help me and not to worry. My dad had to hold my mom so that she could not hit the doctor, but he couldn't cover her mouth and she called him all sort of names she could think of. She then demanded him to let her stab him repeatedly on his leg without worrying about the pain. Mom was destroyed. She was thinking that all the suffering I had been through had been useless. She could find no comfort.

My mom hated this doctor because he was uncaring and cold. A couple of days later, Clarita told her that Dr. Quintana had phoned her, in tears, because he really wanted to help me. Mom then understood that despite the coldness he had shown, he was a human being with feelings. Then she was able to forgive him.

When I left the hospital, everything was like it all started. My femur was broken and split, and there was little hope to be repaired.

At home, they took really good care of me. One day Abi approached my sister Romi and kissed her forehead. Romi's skin felt hot so Abi asked her: "why didn't you let us know you were feeling sick?" and she replied: "you were with my brother". She has always been like this, willing to sacrifice everything on my account. I love her with all my heart and thank God for giving me such a caring sister.

Everything indicated that if Dr. Quintana could think of a solution to solve my problem, I would have to be re-operated.

The sores opened up again because I kept on rubbing them in spite of the foam. My parents cut the plastic bandage away and started with the horrible treatments again.

Family and friends came often to visit. They brought me tins of high caloric drinks, cushions, toys, teddy bears and cards with expressions of good will and love.

A priest also came to give me the anointing of the sick sacrament and he said some beautiful words that comforted us.

He told my mom to ask the Virgin Mary for strength, because both shared the pain a mother feels for a child in agony. He added something which I liked very much: "See Jesus in your child and every time you tend to him, you will be tending and helping Jesus, and such a thought will bring you joy". It really seemed to work. From that day on, all the pain and suffering became easier and both our days seemed to go much faster.

Everybody was trying to come up with ideas to help me. Some friends went as far as to investigate a new product for fractures. It couldn't be used on me because my bones were still growing. Therefore Mom and Dad decided to keep me as still as possible, to see if my bones might stick together even with the minimum contact between them. I spent weeks on a seat with sheepskin to prevent sores from forming on my back. My mom made a pillow with birdseeds because somebody told her they were good at preventing sores on skin.

A friend of Mom suggested a pain clinic, located at a prominent hospital in Mexico City. My parents thought this sounded like a good idea and took me there. The case was difficult. The doctors didn't know what to suggest. They mentioned a catheter into my spinal column with medication to relax my muscles but discarded this option because it couldn't be used for a long period of time. A neurosurgeon proposed a stimulator in the brain to impede my body's movements so that my femur could heal. It seemed to be the only solution that might work. The mere idea of a brain operation seemed terrible, but my problem was seemed to originate from there. It was a very expensive operation. It involved a chip connected to a computer which sent electric impulses to the place in the brain that generated the involuntary movements.

It was a difficult decision to make not only because of the very high risk and price of the operation but also because the doctors could not guarantee the result. The Clinic sent me to a bone specialist for more X-rays. My bones were further away from each other than before. My being still and, in the same position had served for no purpose. My bones were never going to heal!

We finally went back home and my parents were weighing their options. They didn't really want a brain surgery, although it seemed to be the only way out, they did not want to see me suffer any more. They thought of organizing lotteries or raffles similar to the ones they did when we had to go to Philadelphia They knew their friends and family would help them whenever they needed. My mom managed to get a "free" MRI at the social security clinic because it was necessary to place the chip at exactly the correct spot in the brain.

My sister, Romi, had not yet celebrated her birthday, so Mom and Dad decided to have a small party in her honor at my grandpa's ranch. She was very happy as she was going to play with her friends and ride the new horse my dad had given her a few months back. The eve of the party, Mom and my aunt Aida, were chatting and decided to phone my great grandmother. I could hear them because I was still awake; I was not feeling well and started to moan for Mom to come to my side. My mom said a quick good-bye to her grandma; unaware that it would be the last time she would hear her voice.

My Abi Bere phoned the next morning and told my mom and auntie that her mother had died in her sleep the night before. She asked them not to cancel the party for my sister. They were very sad, but they celebrated with my sister and didn't say one word until the party was over. They had to leave that night and go to Mexico City for the funeral. Romi went from great happiness to absolute sadness because she loved our great grandmother very much. Her birthday party had been clouded by sadness this year and she didn't know what was going to happen on the following one.

My appointment for the MRI was a week later and my grandma Bere and my great grandfather Vicente came this time to look after Romi, so my parents could take me. We had a very early appointment, so they figured we could go and return the same day, even if it took three hours each way.

We arrived in time for the appointment but unfortunately they couldn't perform the MRI because they had forgotten a very "small" detail: no metal was allowed in the magnetic field of the machine and I had three large pins inside my leg. I wonder how nobody thought of that! We got home quite frustrated and tired after this unproductive trip. We made a new appointment for the MRI but first I had to be operated on again to remove the pins.

This time it was easier. They closed my wounds and put the cushion of foam and my plastic bandage on once again. They removed the pins and left the femur broken. To avoid the opening of my ulcers again, my parents immediately removed the bandage and the foam around my hip-joint. With the new cast, my body found another way to hurt itself. Dr. Quintana had left the bandage a bit longer and it almost covered my feet. I found that if I moved my toes upwards, the edge of the bandage would hurt me. Once my body discovered this, it started to move my toes and I was hurting and crying because I could not stop it. Thank God, my dad realized what was happening and shortened the bandages. Unfortunately I had already injured my toes and had new wounds to heal.

Family and friends were always interested and we knew they were praying for me. We asked them to keep on praying because only a miracle could save me.

By that time, Juan Diego, who was the small Indian boy to whom the Virgin of Guadalupe appeared, was about to be canonized a saint. My mom's friends started to pray and asked him to please help me and intercede in my favor before God. They promised to become His very devout followers if only I could get well.

A neighbor gave me a scapular medal and told us it was miraculous. My parents stuck it on my cast.

The day for the MRI finally arrived. This time, my sister, my parents and I left our home town and we stopped at my grandparents', Bere and Arturo, and left my sister with them. My grand dad was desolated and sad. I heard him tell a friend that he was filled with sadness because his grandson was "crucified".

We went directly to the hospital, and we didn't have to wait for very long. This time only Dad went inside with me and Mom waited outside. I had to be put to sleep to go for the MRI. One of the technicians thought that with all the cast and bandages, besides my legs set apart, I might not fit inside the machine, and he was right. They measured my cast and bandage and then the length in the tunnel of the machine. It was just about six inches short, I didn't fit. Since the test takes a long time and they had scheduled the machine for other tests, they told Dad he had ten minutes to solve the problem. It was a feat almost impossible to accomplish! Dad and I left the room and Mom was very surprised to see us coming out so soon. My dad explained and told her we had ten minutes to cut the cast and bandage off my feet so I could fit into the machine.

My dad rushed out and went into a hospital which was next door. He asked the receptionist if there was a bone specialist at the hospital. She replied that there was one, but not in, not at the time. Then she pointed at a man who was walking out of the hospital and told my dad that he was also a bone specialist. Dad ran after him and told him about our problem. He asked him for help to be able to cut the cast and bandage. Without any further explanation, the doctor accepted and Dad came and picked us up. We ran to the doctor's office, he was already waiting with the electric saw to cut the excess piece. It took him one minute to do it and we went running back to the lab. The technicians could not believe we had done it within the "grace" period they had given us. They couldn't turn us away, because we had achieved "the impossible".

People who have been to a trauma clinic in Mexico understand why I say "impossible". Just to see a specialist, usually you have to wait for a scheduled appointment and then you have to be at the doctor's office waiting for your turn. If no emergency occurs and the doctor doesn't have to leave his office to get to the operating room, fine; otherwise all appointments are delayed and you have to come back another time. To have found a specialist who didn't demand to see the X-rays or records and who was willing to believe us... was a "miracle", and to do it in a period of less than ten minutes should also be considered that!

We went to my grandparents' house to pick up my sister. A friend of Dad's asked him to pick up a puppy on our way back home. He wanted to give him to us. Mom didn't want to do it but Dad told her it was not far. He decided to go where the puppy was. While on our way, my sister started to feel sick and had to go to the bathroom, she had diarrhea. Dad finally found a place to stop on the highway. It took us more than two hours to get to the town to pick up the puppy. We had to stop every ten minutes for my sister, so that a trip of three hours turned out to take more than six, with a child in a cast from the waist down, a girl with diarrhea and a puppy. My mom was furious. She believed a dog was not as important to have the family go through such an ordeal. We finally made it back home and could relax.

My health improved, my sores were almost closed and didn't hurt as much. I would still sweat a lot but I was eating more and drinking lots of water. I was feeling better. The results of the MRI were ready and available and we had an appointment with the neurosurgeon to talk about the brain operation.

He explained that in the brain there is a specific place where involuntary movements are generated. He said the stimulator would make them stop. It had to be placed at the precise spot with the help of the MRI because its location is measured in millimeters. A hole is drilled through the skull and the chip is placed in the right area. Once it's in, a series of tests have to be done, and with the computer's aid, the intensity of the electric impulses are measured. The stimulator sends electric information to the brain. It has to be done several times to find the exact amount of electricity that renders the best result because each individual is different. I would have had to stay in the hospital for observation until the exact pattern was found. When he finished his explanation, he told my parents the cost of the operation. Mom and Dad were willing to find the money, but they were not absolutely sure about the surgery because the doctor said that this procedure was excellent in most cases, but couldn't guarantee to be successful in my case, since we didn't have a diagnosis of my disorder nor had an explanation for my movements, he said he could not foresee the consequences.

My parents decided to "think about it" because they knew that nothing which had been considered good for everybody had worked on me. For the time being it seemed to be the "only" solution available.

My parents decided to go for a special retreat for couples, since I was much better. My Abi and Aunt Aida said they would take care of Romi and me.

I felt fine even though my parents were not with me, because my Abi, and my aunt were very loving and caring. Everything was fine but all of a sudden that Saturday I started to have diarrhea. It was a big challenge to keep me clean. My poop was almost impossible to clean; it got in between the plastic bandage and the foam. They did the best they could, but my diarrhea would go to the most impossible places to clean. They didn't want to bother my parents because they knew that they needed some time alone. Every time I got dirty, they were tempted to call them. Finally Sunday came and my parents were picking us up. My stomach was better and I was very happy to see my parents and to go home.

Nothing particular happened for a week. I was still with the bandages and waiting for a "miracle".

My granny Bere told my mom on Friday July 12, that her astrologist had said that on the 13th all my problems would be solved. My mom said this lady had definitely no idea of what was going on. She knew my femur was split in two and we didn't have the money for the brain surgery.

On Saturday my mom was changing my diapers when she saw something moving on the bed cover, it was a worm. She thought it was odd to find such a creature on my bed. She hesitated, thinking how it had gotten there. I can still remember the frightened look on her face. She knew about my diarrhea and got the chills. She knew that the poop that hadn't been cleaned up had created a perfect environment for worms, and she was right.

She ran to call the doctor and explained. He told her that I would need the bandage removed as soon as possible. He couldn't do it until late afternoon. He had a busy day as usual. He suggested I get an X-ray. I was very distressed when I understood that the "tickling" I had been feeling for a couple of days was due to worms under the bandage.

Mom phoned Dad and they took me to get my X-ray. Dad took it to the hospital where doctor Quintana was about to enter the operating room. He read the X-rays and was surprised; he said it had not come out very clear, so he wanted the plastic bandages removed and another X-ray taken. He thought my bone had healed.

I started to cry as loud as possible so as to tell my parents that I was afraid and the idea of worms creeping inside my bandage made me sick

Dad started to remove the plastic bandage. He took a pair of gardening scissors and started to cut as fast as he could. Every minute that passed felt like an hour. It was a difficult task because there was layer after layer of the plastic bandage and he could only cut one layer at a time. Mom was standing by, looking scared and thinking of what she was going to find underneath once the bandages were removed. The girl that helped Mom clean the house was standing with a large black plastic garbage bag to put the bandage that had trapped me for three months.

It took forever for my dad to cut all the bandages. He cut along my thighs and ankles, to cut the bandage in half (lengthwise) and to be able to remove it like the lid of a box.

It took him about two hours. The plastic bandage was resistant, but Dad was determined to finish and help me get rid of such a nightmare; the constant rubbing of the scissors against his fingers, created blisters. He thought it was nothing compared to what I had suffered and never stopped, until the bandage was ready to open.

He had to wait just a bit longer so Mom could get a hold of herself. She was terrified by the idea of the worms. She said that she couldn't do it. She was supposed to remove the cast while Dad would hold me, to place me on my seat so I could stay as still as possible.

Mom, who is usually very courageous, would not dare open the bandage, she kept on screaming. When she saw me crying desperately, she fought against her fear and decided to follow my example of bravery. When she moved the lower portion of the bandage a little bit, a big, fat worm filled with poop, fell on the bed. It was white but had a brown belly because it was stuffed with the poop it had eaten. She felt sick and started to scream again. Seeing me so stressed out, she decided to pull the top part of the bandage and closing her eyes threw it into the big black trash bag. They changed my diaper and carefully sat me down.

They threw everything away, it wasn't that bad. The worms were hidden between the cast and foam of my bandage. It was only when they crept out that I could feel them on my skin.

The feeling of freedom was very strange. After three months of having lead like legs, it felt as if they were floating. They felt like feathers and all my joints hurt. It was like my legs wanted to escape upwards trying to reach the ceiling. I felt insecure and even dizzy. I seemed to loose my balance, now that I had nothing to hold me.

I was strapped securely to my seat, and after a while, went to have another X-ray. We went for what became the last X-ray of this nightmare. The radiologist told my parents the bone was crooked but healed. When Dr. Quintana saw it, he was amazed. He took out his digital camera and took a few pictures. He was smiling and stated: "the children's body is a marvelous thing!" but we knew better because we are sure that God is marvelous!

We experienced complete happiness. Our miracle had happened.

My parents let family and friends know what had occurred, they thanked everyone for their prayers and Mom phoned my Abi to share our happiness with her and confirm that the astrologist was right A mass was organized to thank God for His love. All the family was there. It was a beautiful moment. All the kids brought flowers and balloons. Everybody wanted to hug me and I was given a photomontage where Jesus was hugging me. I loved it because I was sure that despite the pain, God had always been there taking care of me...

I still had a little pain but nothing compared with the last months of suffering. I was very happy!

This is the story of how from one day to the next I escaped the three month jail of pain. I think God sent the worms to attract everybody's attention to my bones, to make them aware they had healed. It was unbelievable! This is something I shall never forget.

SIX

About love and compassion

Love is the word that describes my environment to perfection.

I receive love on a daily basis, from my family, friends, teachers and even from strangers.

Compassion is a beautiful feeling. I used to think it was a synonym of pity but I now understand it is an emotion inspired by somebody else's misfortune. It is like trying to be in somebody else's shoes. I don't like to be pitied but I do like to inspire compassion because this feeling brings out the best from the inner part of all human beings.

There are very many different ways to demonstrate compassion and I have experienced them many times in my life.

There are many people who encourage me with words and tell my parents that I am a blessing in their lives. Hundreds of times they have approached me to bring a smile or a tender touch.

On the other hand there are some people who think I am a cross for my parents to bear. Yet some others even avoid looking at me; of these there are few.

I remember a day when a friend of my dad told him, when he learned I was sick, he did not deserve such a thing.

My dad answered: "You are absolutely right; I do not know why God chose me to carry on such an important TASK". He was silenced. Dad has never felt I am his cross to bear or a punishment of God, quite the contrary, he is proud of me.

In general people are friendly and endearing to me, but sometimes they don't know what to say because I cannot answer. This is the majority; but there are people who are talkative and effusive. I believe Sonia wins the prize!

We met her one day we went out to eat. She was the waitress at the restaurant. She came to our table to ask us what we wanted to eat and immediately fell in love with me. She forgot about our order and started to murmur love words to me. She called me "my precious prince", caressed my head and kissed me. My parents and sister were surprised with such demonstrations of love. As Sonia was moving about from table to table and even while being twenty feet away from me, she would shout: "I love you, darling!" and sent me kisses. All the customers were watching an amusing show while eating their food.

When Sonia brought us our food she stayed next to me, caressing me and murmuring baby's words. My parents and Romi could not even eat because they were choking with laughter. They were trying to hide it so they would not offend her. I don't think it would have mattered; she was concentrating on me, loving me. I was also laughing with her.

I only wish people could express their emotion so openly!

Every time we came back to the restaurant she would greet me the same way. Once she stayed at our table and fed me, leaving her customers unattended. It was fun to go there to eat. I loved the way she treated me and the way she would ignore everybody else. I think she was a true and authentic person, not concerned about what people may think. This demonstration of love was very original.

People react in different ways when they are close to me. Sometimes I am surprised of the impact I have in their lives and the way they show it.

I remember the story of my mom's teacher. She had twin children. One of them broke a hand and had to undergo surgery. The anesthesiologist misplaced the intubation and when a complication arose, the oxygen went to his stomach instead of to his lungs, and the child died. She hated the anesthesiologist and wanted to kill him. She charged him with malpractice and tried to send him to jail, but this never happened. She was so depressed that she was thinking of committing suicide without consideration of the other child. One day Mom took me to one of her classes; at this time the teacher was very depressed and considering different plans to kill herself. When she saw me, her eyes filled with tears and she bestowed me her love. She called me "prince" talked to me with sweet words and gave me a couple of cassettes with the music Mom had told her I loved. My mom didn't know anything about her plans until the following day when the teacher confessed and admitted everything she had in mind, and how meeting me had change her perspective of suffering. She said I saved her live.

When my mom told me this story I was very impressed. I could never have imagined I was capable of something so incredible. I was very happy for her. From then on, she stopped her plans of vengeance, forgave the doctor and found inner peace in her heart.

Many people have an impulse to give something the moment they see me. The following are some anecdotes that I will never forget:

This happened when we were on vacation at the beach. Romi was with Dad and were about to ride one of those banana boards that are pulled from a fast boat. A man who was selling shirts came to us to offer his merchandise. When he saw me, he stayed with me and waited for my dad to return from his ride.

He offered Dad one shirt, he thanked him but told the man he didn't want or need anything. This man did not leave. He stayed looking at me with love in his eyes and told my dad that I was an angel living in this earth. He told Mom and Dad that they were like Joseph and Mary taking care of Jesus. He was very touched by my presence and said that to him I was Jesus and that it had been a privilege to meet me. He took one of the shirts he was selling and gave it to Dad. My dad said he could not accept such a present but the man insisted. When Dad saw his emotional state he said he would take if he allowed him to pay for it. The man did not accept a penny and said it was a prize for my dad for taking care of Jesus and it was in my honor that he wanted to give it.

This man was very humble and I am sure he needed the money for his family. The sacrifice was huge, incredible. There are people who have very much and find it hard to share. This man needed the money but didn't think of that; he wanted to please God and he saw Him through me. This was a moving experience that made me very happy. Dad still has the shirt and he loves and uses it on very special occasions.

*

Romi was in kindergarten and the school organized a get together with the local soccer team in our home town. It was a good team and was part of the first division. We all went to the stadium and witnessed the fun parents had with their children and the professional players. When the game ended, everybody joined the teams in the field to get autographs and take some pictures. My parents carried my stroller and I was very happy there.

    The players took pictures with Romi and me. There was one particular player who came to me to say hello. His eyes were filled with tears and told me he wanted to give me something. He asked his team mates if they had brought some souvenirs to give away; but nobody had anything. He insisted he wanted to give me something. He took his shirt off and signed it for me. Other players came and signed it too. I was the envy of the whole school; I had something all children dreamt about. My mother was very thankful for this gesture but didn't know what to do with a smelly, sweaty team shirt. They hung the shirt in my bedroom; it couldn't be washed for fear of losing all the autographs. With time the smell went away and it was a prize to show to whoever came to visit.

*

A lot of people give me medals, icons, prayers, rosaries... I have a collection of these. Most of these gifts are really special. People have given away their most miraculous medals, rosaries and scapular medals blessed by the Pope himself. They have given them to me. This generosity I carry in my heart and am truly grateful.

*

Once we were in church for mass and an elderly lady, about eighty years old, came to me and, on an unstoppable impulse opened her wallet and emptied it to the last penny. She checked it to see if there was nothing left. With her hands full of bills and coins told my parents to buy me something. My parents were surprised, she kept on insisting full of emotion and with tears in her eyes. She wanted to give me all she had. Mom and Dad talked to her and thanked her for her generosity but suggested she should better give me a hug and a kiss instead. She accepted the suggestion and left us with a smile in her face.

*

One Sunday we were at the park where they had a Farmer's Market with all sorts of articles for sale. It was fun to go from booth to booth seeing different merchandise. There were a lot of people and it was difficult to walk fast. We arrived at the kiosk in the center of the park and sat for a while, away from the noise and vendors. There was a sculptor selling some pieces that he carried in a bundle. He offered them while walking. He approached my parents and we thought he was going to try a sale but instead he picked up one piece and told my parents it was special and that he wanted to give it to me for good luck.

    We had already learned that people are very generous and want to give me things. It is very flattering to be so loved.

    We can never repay the love that has been given to me; the time people have volunteered so I could get my therapy, the money given to pay for the high cost of therapy training and the help given to my parents. We would not have been able to achieve all this without all this help and generosity.

In Celaya there was a group called "Grupo Camino" They would do a wonderful job with theater production and the funds they got were used to help someone in need. My second visit to Philadelphia was sponsored by them. They offered two shows to help Daniela, a friend with a cerebral injury, and I. This way we could carry on with our rehabilitation program.

Occasionally help has arrived unexpectedly. One day a girl came to knock at our door and told us she had seen us in church and offered my mom her help with whatever she needed done. Mom didn't have help in the mornings when she had to drive and pick up my sister after school; therefore I used to lie on my bed alone until she could make it back. She used to take the baby, my younger sister Aida with her. There were times she had to wake her up to take her along. Karla, this girl, was a neighbor. She gave us her address and the name of her parents so we could talk to them. Her help was a blessing from heaven! She would come every day to take care of Aida and me while Mom went to pick up Romina. What a beautiful gesture from a sixteen years old girl! She just wanted to help because she was touched when she met me.

Another person who offered her help was the lady concierge at the Dell's Children Hospital in Austin. She met my dad at the hospital and offered her help because she was also a neighbor. She was willing to help whenever she was needed. I felt very happy when I learned I had helped her too by giving her with an important message.

One day before I met her, my school mates and teachers had sent me a plush frog to the hospital wishing me a quick recovery. I have had many animals but this was the first time someone had given me a frog. Mom thought it was very cute and original. They sent the present with two balloons attached to the toy. The doctor came to tell us I could go back home and since Dad was coming to pick us up we had to wait. We emptied my room so another child could use it and went down to the cafeteria to see Dad arrive.

My mom saw my dad talking to a lady, who was the concierge, and who was happy I was going home. We approached them and when Lilly saw my two balloons she told me they were very pretty. She noticed something green on my lap and asked me if it was a doggie. Mom told her it was a frog, and suddenly her eyes were full of tears. I was wondering why a green frog made her so sad but I also thought she was crying maybe because of me as many people do. Lilly explained that the frog was an animal that represented her father and that the following day would be his birthday; but that unfortunately he had passed away very recently.

Mom told her that I was a messenger to let her know that her father was fine and close to her. She became all smiles thinking my mom was right.

SEVEN

In painful transit towards God

The capacity I have to survive is quite impressive! If it were not so, I would have left this world long ago.

Like a curse, my life has experienced threatening events each and every year.

With the peculiar movements of mine, a series of complicated problems, difficult to solve, arose. There was many a time that my parents had to take decisions that were not easy or ordinary.

I started to move from one day to another and still now I am unable to stop. I was only one year old when this strange symptom appeared.

When I was almost two, I started to bite myself as I already mentioned. At the beginning it was as if though my teeth would scratch my mouth, like sucking them to the inside. My lips were swollen and very red. One day I sucked my lips inside my mouth and my teeth clenched and then I experienced pain. This pain was stimulus enough, for me not to stop. Mom and Dad didn't know how to make me stop. They would ask me to open my mouth but my teeth seemed glued together and I was unable to do it although the pain was terrible. Blood would drain from my mouth and there was no way to open it.

When finally my mandibular muscles would relax, I could open my mouth. With the pain I felt, my movements increased and became almost impossible to control.

My mouth went from getting bad to worse, my parents tried to make me stop by holding my lips with their hands. But sometimes my lips would slip from their fingers and I would continue biting.

It got to the point I could not even eat. To put a spoon inside my mouth was quite a battle because I would use it as a support to bite with more strength. I couldn't sleep well because even while sound asleep, my lips seemed to get in between my teeth.

My parents took turns to sleep. There was always one of them to watch for a half hour while the other slept. The one resting felt like he had slept for a minute while the one taking care of me thought it had been an eternity. They would keep a finger inside my mouth, a very uncomfortable position. If they even dozed of for one second, my body would immediately take advantage to continue hurting itself. We were all exhausted!

After a long period of biting, my lower lip changed color and a portion of it died. My mom's worst fear became true. A piece of my lip detached and you could see my teeth through my mutilated mouth.

I had already taken a piece of my lip but yet could not stop biting! When I was biting, my body would arch and my head would turn to a side so my neck was twisted and didn't allow air to get through my trachea. I was constantly choking. I have a short nose and my nostrils shut down when I choke. At first my parents didn't know how to help me because I was not getting any air. One day, Dad thought of closing my mouth and opening my nostrils at the same time with his fingers. He put my head forwards and straight. This is the best way they have found to help me breathe. This has saved my life several times.

I was taken to a dentist but Mom and Dad didn't want me to have my teeth removed, so the dentist made a sort of splint to prevent me from injuring myself. It seemed to help but the relief lasted for about five minutes. That was the time it took my body to find a way to use the splint to hurt itself in a different way. When we left the dentist's office, the splint was no longer served its purpose.

We went to see another dentist, a friend of my dad, Edwin, who later became my godfather when I made my First Communion. He tried very hard to help me. He designed a sort of palate with thick molar covers that impeded the closing of my mouth and therefore my upper teeth didn't touch my lips so I couldn't bite.

Everything seemed to improve for a while, but the second day of wearing it I broke the palate and almost swallowed a piece. Dad arrived just in time to help me. It was midnight and my parents phoned Edwin to ask for his help. He came home several times at odd hours. He would bring the materials he needed and worked on the dinning room table to make another palate and thus free me temporarily of my pain. My mouth started to heal and I started to sleep better. My parents kept on watching me.

One day the palate didn't work any more. Mom saw my face and realized I was in terrible pain. My mouth was clenched and my eyes were opened wide. With the molar covers I started to grind and with this mandibular movement I succeeded in removing the two molars that supported the palate. It was incredible how I always found a way to injure myself.

The situation got even worse, because with my lower teeth I made a large groove in my inner lip. Mom was afraid I would end with no lips at all. There was nothing else to do, my parents had to put their finger inside my mouth and hold my lips at all times.

Just before leaving to Philadelphia, Dad bought a guard; it was similar to the ones boxers wear during their fights. It was made out of rubber and seemed to be a good option. They tried it that night. Dad put the guard on my lower teeth but when I felt it I clenched my mouth with all my might and blood started to pour through my mouth and down my chin. They didn't understand what had gone wrong. When finally Dad and Mom could open my jaw, they saw I had used the guard as a support and had loosened almost all of my lower teeth and they were hanging towards the outside of my mouth. The pain was terrible and I really didn't want to do that. Edwin thought that my teeth would settle later, but it was not so, when we came back from Philadelphia he had to extract them all.

An expert in genetics thought I could be suffering the Lesch-Nyhan Syndrome, just as Dr. Wilkinson from Philadelphia suggested. Mom investigated at the library and was very surprised because many of the symptoms were similar to what was happening to me.

Before anybody suggested that maybe I was possessed, Mom felt there was some force that worked against my will and that forced me to injure myself. She was desperate to see me suffering like that. At times she would shake my body and cry out for this force to leave my body in peace and go away. She would cry anxiously worried because it would not abandon me.

Two months before Romina, my sister was born, my parents went to see mom's gynecologist who confirmed the baby was a girl and my parents felt relieved. Lesch-Nyhan Syndrome is a disease that affects males only, despite the fact that women may be carriers.

The geneticist got us in touch with a group of researchers at the University of Mexico who were studying this disorder. They took some blood from Mom and me and strangely enough, a week later the results were negative.

Romina was born healthy and beautiful.

I was much better after my teeth were removed, but I still kept on trying bite myself.

When I was three years old and was working hard towards my rehabilitation, the nightmare started again. By accident I bit my tongue while doing one of the tumbling exercises and I continued non-stop. The pain I felt was unbearable.

This time it was much worse, my parents tried to hold my tongue but it was more difficult to do than my lip. When they tried to feed me and had to bring out their finger, I chewed my tongue instead of swallowing my food. The adrenaline created by this stress made me vomit and I started to lose weight and blood and thus became very weak.

Mom and Dad took us to the beach to distract me and entertain us. They took along two nannies to help with Romi and prepare food. My parents were dedicated entirely to me.

We stayed there only one day because Mom decided my teeth had to be removed because my life was endangered. We drove for nine hours to come back home, during which Mom couldn't remove her finger from my mouth. It was a very tiresome and what seemed eternal trip.

When we arrived home, Clarita saw me and doubted she could help me through. I needed a blood transfusion before they could operate on me. My blood was very weak and my mouth infection had gone to my kidneys so they had to give a very strong antibiotic. When I finally made it to the operating room, my tongue was almost severed and was attached only by three millimeters. I had managed to cut it lengthwise with the biting edge of my molars. They didn't sew it together; they only removed my molars and two of my canine teeth. Edwin told my parents my tongue would heal by itself.

The following day I started biting the other side of the tongue. They now knew what had to be done. Two days later I was operated on again.

The next year they had to remove the rest of my dental pieces and I was in peace for some time.

A day after they removed all of my teeth; my parents took Romi to a party and I was with them. A small kid stared at me because my gums were all swollen and filled with blood. He asked my dad what had happened to me. Dad told him I had had a sanguinary fight with a crocodile. I thought that joke was fun.

When I was five years old my new molars started to grow. This time a maxillofacial surgeon performed the operation. My molars were deeply attached to the bone.

As my permanent teeth started to grow, they had to remove them one by one. When my front upper teeth came out I was able to keep them since I had no lower ones to hurt myself. I still have four incisors, two canines and two molars. This is good for my self-esteem because when I had no teeth people would stare at me with curiosity.

When I was six years old I was in danger because of an accident.

We were playing outside with Romi, and Mom was pushing my stroller. We were playing "wolf". My stroller hit the curb and one of the tires broke. I ended up hitting my head on the sidewalk. Mom could not pick me up because the stroller was too heavy, neighbors came to help her. My forehead was scratched and I had a huge bump. Dad arrived in five minutes because my mom had phoned and told him what had happened. Thank God I had no fracture and it was only a good scare!

That same year we had a chance to go to New York City for a holiday with all of dad's relatives. We spent Christmas there and started the New Year, it was 2001. It was during this trip that my reflux got worse. When I ate I would choke more than "normal" and the food would come out from my nose and mouth. The heartburn I felt would really burn my insides and that made me very upset.

It was a difficult time because "feeding time" became very dangerous; I would choke and turn black and blue.

Four months went by and one day Mom saw the food I was vomiting looked dark brownish. That day I vomited small amounts of what looked like lentil soup all day long.

Mom asked Clarita if it could be blood and she said "yes".

That same night I started to vomit blood. It was not fresh blood but digested. Mom phoned Clarita and she recommended Dr. Arturo Ramirez, pediatric surgeon. Mom put me to bed. She was going to take me to the doctor the next morning but a few minutes later my pajamas were covered with another vomit. Dad arrived from work and when he saw me, he untied me and told my mom we were going directly to the hospital. They called a neighbor so she could come and baby-sit Romi while my grandparents, Pedro and Coco, came to pick her up.

I threw up quite heavily at the hospital. Dr. Arturo, the surgeon arrived few minutes latter. Clarita had advised him to do a venous dissection for the IV fluid and medicines.

Next morning they took an ultrasound to see the degree of my reflux. They gave me something horrible to drink and they could see on a small screen my digestive system and the amount of fluids that came back.

They also inserted a small camera through my mouth and pushed it all the way to my stomach to see the inside. They took a sample of the tissue.

The results showed that besides a hiatus hernia, my stomach was bleeding because the acidosis had destroyed the mucous layer that covers the stomach's tissue.

My parents were praying to God with all their heart that I didn't have to undergo surgery. Fortunately the problem was resolved with medication.

The following year, during the month of April my hip dislocation was discovered and I went through the two terrible operations I already described.

In April, 2003, when everything seemed to be calm and fine, my uncle Emilio, aunt Aida and cousin Diego, came to visit for Romi's birthday.

At that time I had two strollers. My seat was transferred from one to the other because one was easier to maneuver but was also bigger. According to where we were going we would take one or the other.

For some reason they forgot to tie the Velcro straps that held the chair to the stroller frame. My relatives left and Mom stayed home to look after the children. She was in the bathroom when I started to kick and bang my legs. When I noticed the chair was moving, my body started to move them faster, suddenly I felt the chair falling forward and since I was unable to use my hands, I ended up crashing against the floor with my forehead.

As my mom, sister and cousin, heard the noise, they came to see me. The children helped Mom to lift the heavy chair where I was seated. Dad arrived as soon as possible.

I was very scared and Mom untied me to hold me. Everything went round and round and I threw up. This was a bad symptom. My parents were observing me and saw my eyes moving from one side to the other and then I vomited again.

My uncle and aunt arrived that minute and Mom and Dad took me to the hospital.

This time I was not as lucky as the time the tire of my stroller broke. The X-rays showed a cranial fracture. My head had cracked like an egg!

Clarita put me in hospital for observation. They expected my face to swell ant to turn black and blue; but that was not the case. I left the hospital 24 hours later and went home. I was supposed to stay as still as possible so that the bones would heal in a few weeks.

My dear sister Romi started to believe that her birthday was cursed. Every year she worries about something happening to me.

It had been two days since I had arrived from the hospital when I experienced the incident with my stretchy pajamas that I previously mentioned. Needless to say, I had a fractured skull when I hit my head against the metal board of my bed!

Clarita was very worried; she told my parents that they had to find a way to stop my movements' problem because otherwise she was afraid I was somehow going to end up killing myself.

My parents believed they had tried to find all possible solutions. They re-considered the brain surgery, but they had goose bumps every time they thought about a possible complication.

One day at the doctor's office for a follow up appointment, mom asked Dr, Aguilar if there was another alternative to stop the movement of my legs without taking away their sensibility; the doctor's reply was affirmative. The operation is called selective rhizotomy; it is the disconnection of the root of the nerves in the spinal cord. There are motor and sensory roots, with a special instrument they identify which nerve fibers to cut. This is not a very common surgery, but there are some cases, like mine, that require such a procedure to improve the quality of life.

The neurosurgeon gave my parents the estimate cost of the surgery, it was a very expensive procedure and so my parents asked my two grandparents for help, who immediately agreed.

The surgery was carried out in Mexico City.

I went in the operating room and it took five hours to come out. Dr. Aguilar was also present during the surgery. My left leg was completed disconnected and my right leg had a restricted movement. I could only fold it upwards.

When the nerves are operated on, the neurosurgeon has to take out a piece of bone to let them exposed. This bone has to be kept in a special fluid to be preserved during the hours of operation. Upon the removal of my bone piece, the nurses had to change shifts. Therefore the nurse in charged for putting the bone piece in the fluid, just left. A few minutes later Dr. Aguilar realized what had happened and placed the bone in the solution. When he came out of the operating room, he told my parents he was concerned because there was a possibility of infection, all due to negligence.

When the surgery was over, Dad was waiting for me at the recovery room. He is always allowed in because nobody else knows how to restrain me. I cannot be left alone on a normal stretcher.

The operation had been a success, but Mom was a bit nervous when she saw I could move my right leg. The neurosurgeon informed her he had left some movement because it was better for me. I don't understand why doctors keep all the information to themselves. Once the operation is over, they reveal to the patient the consequences of the action they took.

When in an accident, a person injures his or her bone marrow; they may end up with paralysis. This injury had been done to me on purpose, but my parents were unaware of the possible complications that would arise.

Since the injury was located at the lumbar vertebras, that is to say more or less at your waist area, all the organs that are located below the lesion, may be affected. To begin with, one may end up with bowel and bladder dysfunction. That is what happened to me.

Since I had been given a large amount of IV fluid, the bladder blew up like a balloon and I could not pee. The doctors were aware of this, but my parents did not have the vaguest idea. They placed hot water bags to help me empty my bladder but it stayed full. They had to help me with a catheter to empty it. A few hours later, the bladder started to fill again. It felt really uncomfortable not being able to pee. They tried the bags of hot water again but I was unsuccessful. My parents felt very sad when they thought they would have to use the catheter for the rest of my life. If the bladder is not emptied completely, an infection may occur.

My dad, under Divine inspiration, thought to press down on my bladder and urine started to flow out automatically, without the catheter. This was a great relief because I hated to have the catheter introduced through the hole in my penis.

This is the way my bladder is emptied every day. I thought it was a normal procedure to help people who have lost control of their sphincter, but doctors are always surprised with our exclusive technique.

The operation itself was not really painful, with all the pain medicine I was able to cope.

Dr Aguilar suggested the use of Botox again to finish my treatment. This time he would give me the maximum dosage required for my weight and since he was going to inject only my upper body, he was expecting to get better results. He could not do it while I was sedated. I have to be awake and moving, so that he could tell which muscles needed to be injected.

That night I was very weak and was running a fever due to the surgery but still they injected me with Botox one more time. My Abi was in the room with my mom and she could not stop crying as she was a witness to all the things they were doing to me.

This time the Botox injections worked differently, I was completely relaxed and felt very good.

We went to my grandparents', Arturo and Bere, after being released from the hospital. While my mom was changing my diaper, she noticed something different in my body. My anus was opened and its muscles were completely loose, it was yet another of the consequences of the surgery. This surgery was the cause of loosing my sphincters.

There were some people who criticized my parents for making me go through this operation, but it has been the most peaceful period in my life so far. Since I was not fighting the involuntary jerky movements of my legs, my nerves relaxed and therefore I stopped sweating with anxiety. Now, other people could carry me. I was happy not to struggle with my body all the time. It was an awesome phase of my life.

This happiness didn't last very long, new symptoms appeared. One day my mom noticed something strange with me. My eyes moved from one side to the other constantly and I started feeling very dizzy. She sat me on my chair to feed me breakfast. Everything was moving around, I threw up and fell asleep. I was very weak. Mom put me to bed and I stayed there for hours. Mom injected something for the dizziness but I was feeling the same all day. These unexplainable vertigo scenes still occur at least once or twice a year.

I had undergone the operation for four months and the movement of my right leg kept increasing. I started to recover the mobility that had been eliminated and my battle started again.

The neurologists were absolutely amazed of what was happening to me. There are all sorts of research around the world going on trying to help and enable people who had been paralyzed, to recover some movement. My body had somehow managed to connect the nerve roots that had been severed purposely.

I was very uncomfortable because my leg movement caused pain on my recently operated hip. My parents were very concerned and thought that another rhizotomy would be the only solution to my problem.

The neurosurgeon who had performed the rhizotomy agreed to operate on me again but we had no money to do it.

My parents had to look for another neurosurgeon who worked for the Social Security System.

They asked for help from the National Medical Center, but the neurosurgeon there, did not want to do this type of operation. He wanted to help me but he thought it was a very drastic measure. He ordered many exams because he preferred a brain stimulator.

For one of the tests, they had to put me under. They brought in a portable aspirator and oxygen because there was none in that room. When they placed me inside the tunnel of the machine to perform the test, my mom noticed I was choking. She knew exactly what to do but all the staff was in panic. They aspirated me and gave me oxygen, the test was done very fast because they were very concerned with my reaction.

In order to carry out some more tests and avoid any risks, I was admitted to the hospital again. The only place equipped with all the necessary instruments to monitor my well being was the operating room.

They did a muscle biopsy but there wasn't anybody at the lab to process it. The evoked potentials indicated I was going blind and deaf.

When the neurosurgeon told my parents that brain surgery was not feasible either because my nerves were damaged and my disease was progressive, they had to look for help somewhere else.

The neurologists at the Medical Center prescribed many different medications, but it only served to keep me sedated all day.

Dr. Aguilar recommended another neurosurgeon to perform the rhizotomy. When this doctor saw me, he absolutely refused to operate on me. He also suggested the chip in the brain, because that was his specialty. Mom and Dad explained to him what the other neurosurgeon said about it but he insisted asking them how would they possibly know it wasn't good for me if they didn't even know the diagnosis of my condition? He sent us to Dr. Zenteno, who diagnosed the Hallervorden-Spatz Syndrome. It was then that Dad researched this disorder and discovered my most probable diagnosis.

Nobody wanted to perform the rhizotomy that had greatly helped me. Someone recommended yet another neurosurgeon who also attended a government hospital. We went for our appointment and he immediately said yes, he was willing to help me. He knew all the things that had happened because Mom and Dad had told him.

The day for surgery arrived. There were eight of us sharing a room; we all had different health problems. There was only one person allowed in the room per child. The doctors came to get me and Mom stayed in the room with a broken heart full of despair. My dad somehow managed to enter the room and together they waited for about five hours.

I came back in a stretcher and was placed in my bed. I was extremely restless, and when my mom saw me she wanted to die. The leg that was supposed to be disconnected was moving! We never learned what had been performed at the operating room, but it wasn't what I needed. The movement of my leg had only diminished, but my parents knew it would recover its full movement. The doctors did not answer my parents' questions. They assured them they had cut the nerve roots completely.

That night was a nightmare! My dad was allowed to stay in because they saw how much I was moving. The IV was hurting me and I couldn't find a comfortable position.

Mom could find no consolation. All the pain experienced had been useless. She swore that I would never have to go through such a thing again. She would cry asking for my forgiveness.

The wound in my back was 10 inches long and it hurt a lot. My mom noticed swelling around it but figured it was because it was very recent. I was allowed to go home, and I felt relieved.

The wound was still swollen and the skin around it felt very soft.

One day while Mom was moving me to my chair, she felt my back all wet. She noticed a mixture of blood and water. When she lifted my T-shirt up, she saw that the wound had burst open about 6 inches, exposing the muscle tissue of my back.

She asked the lady who was helping at home for help. Mom tried to keep the wound closed with some small bandages. She took me to see Carlos, the pediatrician, to sew me back up. He couldn't do anything about it; the wound had to close itself...

Days went by and my wound would not heal due to the water discharged from it. I was taken back to the hospital thinking I had a fistula, and if necessary, to operate on me again. I had no fistula and we had only to be patient and wait for the body to heal itself.

The treatment to clean my wound didn't hurt very much. The wound started to close slowly and was completely closed within two months.

As a consequence of my movements, I dislocated my hip bone again and the pain is always there.

The only treatment that seemed to work to keep me still and without pain was Botox. I had to have it every five months.

To get my shots, Dr. Aguilar recommended a therapist in Mexico City because he had moved to another state. Another time we had to travel to the city of Leon, about one hour away from Celaya to get them from a different doctor. Finally Dr. Barrera, who is a plastic surgeon and lived in our home town gave me the injections at no cost and instructed my mom how to do it herself.

2006, I was 12 years old, was a wonderful year free of problems. We arrived in Austin, Texas and since I had no insurance, Mom brought the Botox with her from Mexico and she gave me the injections, exactly as Dr. Barrera had shown her.

As time went by, the effect of Botox lasted less and less, due to the antibodies the body creates.

In 2007 we had an accident.

We were driving to my summer camp, as we turned into a street, Mom heard a loud noise. The strapping used to tie my stroller to the van was not properly secured and made my chair tilt against the door. We could not stop because we were on the freeway. My mom got very nervous and started to talk to me, I was quiet and afraid, sitting on my stroller. Finally, my mom made a turn to get out of this freeway to be able to stop but my stroller crashed against the floor. I had not been hurt because I was well protected in my seat but Mom didn't know if I had hit my head or was unconscious.

When we finally stopped Mom was nervously shaking She ran to see me and tried to lift my stroller but could not because it was very heavy. She placed her thigh under my head, so I would not hit my head against the floor and started to shout out for help. Nobody would stop because they were driving very fast. She tried to lift me again, but to no avail.

A man came on a motorcycle and Mom called him very loudly. He came back to help us, then both of them were able to lift my stroller.

A police car arrived and asked us if we needed help. Mom was shaking so much she could not tie me. The policeman waited patiently for her to finish and then drove ahead of us so we could get back into the Freeway. Nothing serious happened, but the incident was really frightening.

That same year we went to see the specialist in movement disorders in Houston. The medication prescribed provoked different movements and I started to bite my tongue with a canine tooth that had come out a couple of years before.

On a Saturday I started to hurt myself with this tooth, Dad decided to go to Mexico immediately and see my godfather, Edwin. By the time we got there, I had already managed to make a hole in my tongue. On Sunday they phoned the anesthesiologist and on Monday morning the tooth was removed and I could eat and sleep again.

Once the problem was resolved, we came back to Austin to carry our normal routine.

The effect of Botox had already worn out, I needed a new dosage. Mom made an appointment with Dr. Richards, the specialist. They explained my problem to her and took a CD with all my previous files. Dr, Richards agreed to inject the Botox even though she was surprised when my parents told her the doses they usually gave me. She trusted them and injected the highest dosage she had ever used.

I was admitted in hospital to be sedated, this time I didn't feel the shots.

I felt calmed after the shots but unfortunately the effect only lasted for about three weeks. The antibodies in my system were more than ready to get rid of the toxin. The doctor and my parents decided it wasn't worth it for such a short relief.

In January, 2008 I was admitted in the hospital again. That day, Mom sensed a strong ammonia odor coming out of the pee in my diaper, she thought the pee was very concentrated due to the fact it had been there all night long. At mid-morning Crompton called my mom and told her something was wrong with my urine. While changing my diaper at school, they noticed that my urine was very dark. When they pressed down on my stomach to bring out the urine out, it was mixed with blood. My parents came to pick me up along with Romi, so she could take care of my baby sister while we were in the hospital.

I had a bad infection in my urinary track and I frequently felt the urge to push. I was running a high fever and was very weak. I could not stay awake.

I stayed in hospital for treatment. To avoid any problems, they placed the IV fluid in my left foot, the one with no movement. It was hard to do it because my veins there are very thin.

The doctors wondered how I had gotten the infection, because men seldom get it.

Mom knew what had happened. Crompton, who normally changed my diaper, had recently undergone knee surgery. She was recovering, so she was unable to take care of me. For the past week, another of my nice teachers was in charge of my diaper change. She didn't press down on my stomach hard enough to bring out all the pee because she didn't want to hurt me. Therefore, my bladder wasn't properly emptied and bacteria started to grow inside. My teacher felt somewhat responsible for what had happened to me and came to visit me at the hospital. Mom told her it wasn't really her fault because she wasn't aware on how important it was to empty my bladder completely. She also informed my teacher that I was responding very well to all the prescribed antibiotics. Mom was sure this would never happen again.

I only spent two nights at the hospital and was out like new!

When back in school, my teachers were scared to feed me because sometimes I would choke a lot and turn blue. Crompton knew how to make me come out of it.

It was suggested to my parents that it would be a good idea if I could get a tube in my stomach to feed me. All teachers and the nurse at school agreed to this idea because they were afraid something bad could eventually happen to me.

With all this pressure, my parents took me to see a gastroenterologist to get information about the G-tube. They chatted for a long time about it. After the check up, Dr. Behane agreed with my parents. She thought the tube was not necessary and she was also afraid of the possible consequences of how my body could use it as a weapon to hurt itself.

So far I have been well at school and I don't choke as much.

The last problem we had to face had to do with my lower canines. This time we didn't go to Mexico to fix it. After making an appointment with the dentist, Mom talked to me and explained exactly what he was going to do with my teeth. She said that if I was able to cooperate, the dentist would file my canines and flatten them without putting me under. She explained in detail how the drill works and the funny noise it makes.

Dr. Ray was willing to help me. He thought he could make it without putting me under. I was very cooperative, I yelled only a couple of times because the drill inside my mouth felt strange. My mom and a very strong young man held me while the dentist did his job. The task was complete within 30 minutes, we left the dentist office and I felt happy to have flat and smooth canines. My mom told me how proud she was and I felt good to be able to demonstrate some maturity.

This disease seems to add new symptoms every day. During our last vacations at the beach, after a very sunny day, I had my first seizure. I didn't feel anything but Romi knew something bad was happening to me and called Mom and Dad. I woke up and felt extremely tired. The following week I had another seizure. I know my parents are really worried about this new symptom and for me; it really makes me wonder what kind of new challenges await us in the future.

When it comes to overcoming any of my problems, I have an amazing inner strength, but as a paradox, my body is extremely fragile. Any complication can bring me to the end.

I am not afraid of death, quite the contrary; when I have been to a funeral I have not been able to hide my happiness. My parents have sometimes felt embarrassed because there, I have laughed really loudly, I am certain there is an after- life.

I don't know if a next crisis will be definite or if I will be able to surpass a lot more. I don't know when I will have to go back to the place where I accepted the task of this disorder, not knowing it was going to be so hard.

The only thing I am absolutely sure is that my reward there will be magnificent and eternal.

The challenge of living has been worth it.
A soul trapped in such a small prison has found the meaning of its existence.
All the love received has compensated so much pain.
Many people see in me an angel because they feel my soul is clean. They like to ask me to pray for them. They think I am close to God. Many have approached me, from different nationalities and religions, also to pray for me. God is the same for all, no matter what our beliefs are.
Faith is a powerful energy and it can make incredible things happen.
I love to pray for others because this is the best way to give them something. I wish I could do more than this, but I have found in prayer the true love for others.
I like to touch the hearts of the people around me and to be able to demonstrate that you can be happy even under the most difficult circumstances.
Happiness is within our heart and it depends on the meaning you give to your life.
It is better to be able to enjoy the things you own rather than living dreaming on what we want to have.

Along with all the things I've been through in my life, there is one thing that's very clear in my mind.
The problems are not important, neither all the hard situations that we encounter. We have to trust in God; because everything, absolutely everything, has an important purpose at the end.

Ivonne Montellano was born in Mexico City. She got her degree in food chemistry from La Salle University. She's been a home stayed Mom for her three children. She actually lives in Austin, Texas with her family and works as a special needs seamstress.

Visit her blog at
http://ivonnemontellano-extraspecial.blogspot.com

We want to read your comments.